ETHNIC BOOK AWARDS:

A DIRECTORY OF MULTICULTURAL LITERATURE FOR YOUNG READERS

SHERRY YORK

Linworth Books

Professional Development Resources for K-12
Library Media and Technology Specialists

Dedication

This book is dedicated to the memory of Gloria Anzaldúa (1942-2004) and of Dr. Abelardo Baeza (1944-2004), two Tejanos whose teaching, writing, and dedication to literature and justice influenced me profoundly.

Acknowledgments

Thanks again to Donna Miller, fellow librarian and friend; to Marlene Woo-Lun; and to my husband, Donnie, my life's companion and dearest friend.

Library of Congress Cataloging-in-Publication Data

York, Sherry, 1947-
   Ethnic book awards : a directory of multicultural literature for young readers / Sherry York.
   p. cm.
   Includes indexes.
   ISBN 1-58683-187-9 (pbk.)
   1. Children's literature, American--Bibliography. 2. Young adult literature, American--Bibliography. 3. Multiculturalism in literature--Bibliography. 4. Ethnic groups in literature--Bibliography. 5. Children's literature, American--Awards. 6. Young adult literature, American--Awards. I. Title.

Z1037.A2Y67 2005
011.62--dc22
                              2005004332

Author: Sherry York

Linworth Books:
Carol Simpson, Editorial Director
Judi Repman, Associate Editor

Published by Linworth Publishing, Inc.
480 East Wilson Bridge Road, Suite L
Worthington, Ohio 43085

ISBN: 1-58683-187-9

5 4 3 2 1

Table of Contents ————————————

Introduction

Since 1968 several culturally-specific awards have been developed to recognize excellence in children's and young adult books. These awards identify high-quality books about Jewish, African-American, Latino, Caribbean, and Asian-American cultures. The Sydney Taylor, Coretta Scott King, Carter G. Woodson, Américas, Tomás Rivera, Pura Belpré, and Asian Pacific American Awards publicize books with outstanding content that reflects the existence and value of ethnic and cultural diversity in our contemporary society.

Librarians and educators who realize the importance of conveying the message that all ethnic groups in our society have value and who understand that children's book authors and illustrators who are members of minority ethnic groups have much to offer will find this index a useful resource. Part I provides background information about ethnic book awards. Part II is an alphabetical listing of books that are award winners and are honor or commended titles. Publication information and brief summaries are provided for the titles in Part II. A subject index and an index of authors, editors, illustrators, and translators provide several points of access.

Librarians and library media specialists can use this book as a tool for selection and acquisition of high-quality books to increase diversity in library collections. Although information about each of the awards is available on the Internet, searching for, obtaining, and compiling that information is a time-consuming process.

Classroom teachers can use this index to locate worthy books to supplement classroom instruction. Educators may wish to browse and compile personal reading lists to learn more about various cultural groups. As our society grows increasingly multicultural, it is vitally important that educators recognize and celebrate cultural differences and similarities as we educate and inspire our students.

Students of children's literature should find this book a useful resource for learning about multicultural children's and young adult literature. By using *Newbery & Caldecott Awards: A Subject Index* (Linworth, 2003) and *Capturing Readers with Children's Choice Book Awards: A Directory of State Programs* (Linworth 2004), and this book, students will be able to quickly and easily access information about hundreds of award-winning books!

I hope that librarians in all types of libraries and educators in many settings will use this index as a tool with which to reach out to ethnic patrons and students and show respect for their cultures. I also hope that educators and librarians will use this book to increase and showcase diversity in children's and young adult literature for all pupils and patrons, regardless of ethnicity.

PART I:
THE AWARDS

1968 Sydney Taylor Book Award
  <www.jewishlibraries.org/ajlweb/awards/st_books
  .htm>
1970 Coretta Scott King Award
  <www.ala.org/ala/emiert/corettascottkingbookawards/
  corettascott.htm>
1974 Carter G. Woodson Award
  <www.socialstudies.org/awards/writing/>
1993 Américas Award
  <www.uwm.edu/Dept/CLACS/outreach/americas.html>
1995 Tomás Rivera Mexican American Children's Literature Award
  <www.education.txstate.edu/subpages/tomasrivera/>
1996 Pura Belpré Award
  <www.ala.org/ala/alsc/awardsscholarships/literaryawds/belpremedal/
  belprmedal.htm>
2001 Asian Pacific American Award for Literature (APAAL)
  <www.apalaweb.org/awards/awards.htm>

The **Sydney Taylor Book Award** was established in 1968 in honor of the author of the *All-of-a-Kind Family* book series published between 1951 and 1978 about the life of an Orthodox Jewish family. The award encourages publication of outstanding books of positive Jewish content for children. Awards are selected by a committee of the Association of Jewish Libraries and recognize "distinguished contributions to Jewish children's literature." Two awards are given each year, for younger readers and for older readers. Honor books are also recognized.

The **Coretta Scott King Award** established in 1970 commemorates the life and work of Dr. Martin Luther King, Jr. and honors his widow, Coretta Scott King. The annual award is presented by the Coretta Scott King Task Force, part of the Social Responsibilities Round Table of the American Library Association. According to the Web site, the awards hope to "promote, recognize, and celebrate the continued publication of quality literature by African-American children's authors and illustrators." Winners and honor books are recognized.

The **Carter G. Woodson** multicultural award was established in 1973 by the National Council for the Social Studies, Racism and Social Justice Committee. In honor of an African-American historian, educator, and writer, this award recognizes exemplary books written for children and young people that "respect ethnic and racial differences." Awards are conveyed annually for elementary, middle level, and secondary grade levels.

The **Américas** award began in 1993 and recognizes U.S. works of fiction, poetry, folklore, or nonfiction, in English or Spanish, that "authentically and engagingly portray Latin America, the Caribbean, or Latinos in the United States." Sponsored by the Consortium of Latin American Studies Programs (CLASP) at the Center for Latin American and Caribbean Studies of the University of Wisconsin-Milwaukee, this annual award recognizes a winner, honorable mention, and commended titles. Titles are selected for "distinctive literary quality; cultural contextualization; exceptional integration of text, illustration and design; and potential for classroom use."

The **Tomás Rivera Mexican American Children's Literature Award** was established in 1995 in honor of educator Tomás Rivera, author of the bilingual novel, *y no se lo tragó la tierra/And the Earth Did Not Part* (Quinto Sol, 1971). This annual award recognizes authors and illustrators who "authentically reflect the lives of Mexican-American children and young adults in the Southwestern region of the United States." Books which may be fiction or nonfiction, written for children or young adults, should accurately portray Mexican Americans without stereotyping, and must be of highest quality.

The **Pura Belpré** award established in 1996 is named for the first Latina librarian at the New York Public Library. A Puerto Rican by birth, Belpré was an author, storyteller, and librarian. This award is co-sponsored by the Association for Library Service to Children (ALSC), a division of the American Library Association, and by REFORMA, the National Association to Promote Library and Information Services to Latinos and the Spanish-speaking. Awarded biennially, the award recognizes a Latino/Latina writer and illustrator, "whose work best portrays, affirms, and celebrates the Latino cultural experience in an outstanding work of literature for children and youth."

The **Asian Pacific American Award for Literature** (APAAL), sponsored by the Asian/Pacific American Librarians Association, was presented in 2001 and 2004. It recognizes meritorious books "by or about" Asian Pacific Americans and is sponsored by the Asian/Pacific American Librarians Association.

A few other ethnic-based awards are in the developmental stages. If "ethnic" authors continue to publish outstanding books for young readers, perhaps the American Indian Library Association and other cultural groups will also establish book awards to recognize diversity in the United States, our complex multicultural country.

PART II:
THE BOOKS

na = not available
oop = out of print
Reading and interest levels are listed as grade levels, with reading
   level first, followed by interest level: RL/IL

A Is for the Americas by Cynthia Chin-Lee and Terri de la Peña.
Enrique O. Sánchez, ill. Orchard, 1999. oop. 6.3/K-3
An alphabetical introduction to the history, geography, and culture of
the Americas.
Américas Commended 1999

Abuela's Weave by Omar S. Castañeda. Enrique O. Sánchez, ill. Lee &
Low, 1993. 2.0/K-3, 4.0/3-6
A Guatemalan girl and grandmother weave special creations and go to
a market to sell them.
Américas Commended 1993

Africa Dream by Eloise Greenfield. Carole Byard, ill. Crowell, 1977.
3.0/P-2
A child's dreams are filled with images of the people and places of
Africa.
Coretta Scott King Winner, Author and Illustrator 1978

The Afterlife by Gary Soto. Harcourt, 2003. 7.0/7-12
A high school senior lives on as a ghost after his murder in the
restroom of a dance club.
Américas Commended 2003

Aïda by Leontyne Price. Leo Dillon, ill. and Diane Dillon, ill. Harcourt, 1990. 2.0/K-3, 5.1/3-6
Verdi's opera in which the love of an enslaved Ethiopian princess for an Egyptian general brings tragedy.
Coretta Scott King Winner, Illustrator 1991

Alejandro's Gift by Richard E. Albert. Sylvia Long, ill. Chronicle Books, 1994. 5.0/P-2
Lonely in his house in the desert, Alejandro builds an oasis to attract animals.
Américas Commended 1994

All Night, All Day: A Child's First Book of African American Spirituals by Ashley Bryan. Musical arrangements by David Manning Thomas. Atheneum, 1991. 2.0/K-3, 5.0/3-6
Twenty spirituals, distinctive music from the time of slavery.
Coretta Scott King Honor, Illustrator 1992

All the Colors of the Race by Arnold Adoff. John Steptoe, ill. Lothrop, 1982. oop. na/4-8, na/7-9
Poems from the point of view of a child with a black mother and a white father.
Coretta Scott King Honor, Illustrator 1983

Almost to Freedom by Vaunda Micheaux Nelson. Colin Bootman, ill. Carolrhoda Books, 2003. 2.0/K-3
Escape from slavery via the Underground Railroad, from the perspective of a rag doll.
Coretta Scott King Honor, Illustrator 2004

Alphabet City Ballet by Erika Tamar. HarperCollins, 1996. 4.0/3-6
Living in a poor Puerto Rican family complicates life for Marisol when she realizes that pursuing her love for ballet may expose her brother to danger.
Américas Commended 1996

The Always Prayer Shawl by Sheldon Oberman. Ted Lewin, ill. Boyds Mills Press, 1994. 3.0/K-3, 4.0/3-6
A prayer shawl is handed down from grandfather to grandson in this story of Jewish tradition and the passage of generations.
Sydney Taylor Winner, Younger 1994

American Indians Today: Issues and Conflicts by Judith Harlan. Lerner, 1987. oop. na/9-12
Economic, legal, health, and civil rights problems facing Native Americans.
Carter G. Woodson Outstanding Merit 1988

Ancient Israelites and Their Neighbors: An Activity Guide by Marian Broida. Chicago Review Press, 2003. 4.0/4-8
Ancient cultures of the Israelites, Philistines, and Phoenicians.
Sydney Taylor Honor, Older 2003

Andrew Young: Man With a Mission by James Haskins. Lothrop, 1979. oop. na/9-12
Biography of a clergyman, civil rights worker, legislator, and ambassador to the United Nations.
Coretta Scott King Honor, Author 1980

Angel's Kite/La estrella de Angel by Alberto Blanco. Rodolfo Morales, ill. Dan Bellm, trans. Children's Book Press, 1994. 2.0/K-3
A boy makes a kite that restores a long-missing bell to the town church.
Américas Commended 1994

Angela Weaves a Dream: The Story of a Young Maya Artist by Michéle Solá. Jeffrey Jay Foxx, ill. Hyperion, 1997. oop. 6.6/3-7, 6.6/4-6
Photo-essay of a Mayan girl learning the process of weaving.
Américas Commended 1997

Angels Ride Bikes and Other Fall Poems/Los Ángeles Andan en Bicicleta y otros poemas de otoño by Francisco X. Alarcón. Maya Christina González, ill. Children's Book Press, 1999. 2.0/K-3
Bilingual poems celebrating memories of fall in the city and growing up in Los Angeles.
Américas Commended 1999

Anthony Burns: The Defeat and Triumph of a Fugitive Slave by Virginia Hamilton. Knopf, 1988. 5.8/5-8
Biography of the slave whose escape and trial caused a furor between abolitionists and those determined to enforce Fugitive Slave Acts.
Coretta Scott King Honor, Author 1989

Anthony Reynoso: Born to Rope by Martha Cooper and Ginger Gordon. Clarion, 1996. 3.0/3-6
Tony's experiences in the Mexican trick roping tradition handed down to him by his father, grandfather, and great-grandfather.
Américas Commended 1996

Apple Pie 4th of July by Janet S. Wong. Margaret Chodos-Irvine, ill. Harcourt, 2002. 3.0/K-3
A Chinese-American child fears that the food her parents are preparing to sell on the Fourth of July will not be eaten.
Asian Pacific American Winner, Illustration 2004

Arctic Explorer: The Story of Matthew Henson by Jeri Ferris. Carolrhoda Books, 1989. 6.2/5-8
Biography of the black explorer who discovered the North Pole.
Carter G. Woodson Outstanding Merit, Elementary 1990

Ashley Bryan's ABC of African American Poetry by Ashley Bryan. Atheneum, 1997. 2.0/K-3
Letters of the alphabet are represented by lines of poems by African-American poets.
Coretta Scott King Honor, Illustrator 1998

Asphalt Angels by Ineke Holtwijk. Wanda Boeke, trans. Front Street Press, 1999. 4.0/7-12, 8.0/7-12
Abandoned on the streets of Rio de Janeiro, Alex joins a group of street children and adapts to his new life.
Américas Commended 1999

Atlas of Asian-American History by Monique Avakian. Facts on File, 2002. na/9+
History of Asian Americans in the U.S.
Carter G. Woodson Honor, Secondary 2003

Baby's Bris by Susan Wilkowski. Judith Friedman, ill. Kar-Ben Copies, 1999. 2.0/K-3, 4.0/3-6
Sophie becomes a big sister and, during the first days of her brother's life, learns about the custom of bris (circumcision) and celebrates the event with her family.
Sydney Taylor Honor, Younger 1999

Bagels from Benny by Aubrey Davis. Dušan Petričic, ill. Kids Can Press, 2003. 2.0/K-3
Benny, who helps out in his grandpa's bakery, leaves a bag of bagels in the synagogue each week for God, but discovers a man in a tattered coat is eating them.
Sydney Taylor Winner, Younger 2003

Barbara Jordan: Speaking Out by James Haskins. Dial, 1977. oop. na/ya
Biography of the first black Congresswoman from the South.
Coretta Scott King Honor, Author 1978

Barrio: José's Neighborhood by George Ancona. Harcourt Brace, 1998. 3.0/3-6, 4.0/3-6
A boy living in a barrio in San Francisco describes his school, recreation, holidays, and family.
Américas Winner 1998   Pura Belpré Honor, Illustration 2000

Barrio Streets, Carnival Dreams: Three Generations of Latino Artistry edited by Lori Carlson. Henry Holt, 1996. oop. na/ya
Latino literature celebrating the contributions of three generations of twentieth-century Americans of Mexican, Caribbean, and South American descent.
Américas Commended 1996

Baseball in April, and Other Stories by Gary Soto. Harcourt, 1990, 2000. 4.0/3-6, 5.1/5-8
Short stories focusing on the everyday adventures of Latino young people in California.
Pura Belpré Honor, Narrative 1996

Baseball in the Barrios by Henry Horenstein. Harcourt Brace, 1997. 4.9/K-3, 4.9/3-6
Hubaldo, a fifth grader in a barrio in Venezuela loves that country's most popular sport, its teams, and players.
Américas Commended 1997

The Bat Boy & His Violin by Gavin Curtis. E. B. Lewis, ill. Simon & Schuster, 1998. 2.0/K-3, 4.1/3-6
Reginald is more interested in practicing violin than in his father's job managing the worst team in the Negro Leagues, but then his music leads the team to victory.
Coretta Scott King Honor, Illustrator 1999

The Battle of Jericho by Sharon M. Draper. Atheneum Books for Young Readers, 2003. 4.7/3-6
A high school junior and his cousin suffer the ramifications of joining what seemed to be a reputable school club.
Coretta Scott King Honor, Author 2004

Battlefields and Burial Grounds: The Indian Struggle to Protect Ancestral Graves in the United States by Roger C. Echo-Hawk and Walter R. Echo-Hawk. Lerner, 1994. 9.8/6-12, 9.8/6-12
Efforts of Native Americans to rebury ancestral human remains and grave offerings held by museums and historical societies.
Carter G. Woodson Outstanding Merit, Secondary 1995

Bayard Rustin: Behind the Scenes of the Civil Rights Movement by James Haskins. Hyperion, 1997. oop. na/5-8, na/8-12
Biography of a skillful organizer of the U.S. civil rights movement.
Coretta Scott King Honor, Author 1998

Beacon Hill Boys by Ken Mochizuki. Scholastic, 2002. 5.1/7-12, 7.1/7-12
In 1972 Seattle, a Japanese-American teenager struggles for his own identity, along with a group of friends who share his anger and confusion.
Asian Pacific American Honor, Text 2004

A Bear for Miguel by Elaine Marie Alphin. Joan Sandin, ill. HarperCollins, 1996. 3.0/K-3
A girl in El Salvador goes to the market with her father and helps obtain necessities by trading a precious item.
Américas Commended 1996

Beat the Story Drum, Pum-Pum by Ashley Bryan. Atheneum, 1980, 1987. 4.0/3-6
Five Nigerian folktales.
Coretta Scott King Winner, Illustrator 1981

Beautiful Blackbird by Ashley Bryan. Atheneum Books for Young Readers, 2003. 2.0/K-3
Colorful birds of Africa ask blackbird, the most beautiful, to decorate them with his blackening brew.
Coretta Scott King Winner, Illustrator 2004

Because We Are by Mildred Pitts Walter. William Morrow, 1983. oop. na/9-12
After a misunderstanding with a white teacher, black honor student Emma is transferred from the integrated to a segregated high school.
Coretta Scott King Honor, Author 1984

Before We Were Free by Julia Alvarez. Knopf, 2002. 5.6/7-12, 8.0/7-12
In 1960s Dominican Republic, Anita learns that her family is involved in the underground movement to end the bloody rule of General Trujillo.
Américas Winner 2002   Pura Belpré Winner, Narrative 2004

Behind the Mountains by Edwidge Danticat. Orchard, 2002. 5.6/5-8, 8.0/7-12
Writing in the notebook her teacher gave her, Celiane describes life in Haiti and experiences in Brooklyn after the family immigrates.
Américas Honorable Mention 2002

The Bells of Christmas by Virginia Hamilton. Harcourt, 1989. 3.5/3-6, 4.0/3-6
Jason describes the 1890 Christmas that he and his family celebrate in Ohio.
Coretta Scott King Honor, Author 1990

Benjamin Banneker, Genius of Early America by Lillie Patterson. David Scott Brown, ill. Abingdon, 1978. oop. na/9-12
Biography of the distinguished eighteenth-century black astronomer, farmer, mathematician, and surveyor.
Coretta Scott King Honor, Author 1979

Berchick by Esther Silverstein Blanc. Tennessee Dixon, ill. Volcano Press, 1989. 3.0/K-3, 3.0/3-6
Homesteading in Wyoming in the early 1900s, a Jewish mother develops an unusual relationship with a colt she adopts.
Sydney Taylor Winner, Younger 1989

Beyond the Ancient Cities by Jose María Merino. Helen Lane, trans. Farrar, Straus & Giroux, 1994. oop. na/6-10
Miguel, son of a conquistador, embarks on a journey to Panama with his godfather.
Américas Commended 1994

Beyond the High White Wall by Nancy Pitt. Scribner's, 1986. oop. na/6-9
Witnessing the murder of a peasant in the Russian Ukraine in 1903, Libby triggers hate against her Jewish family, prompting them to consider emigrating.
Sydney Taylor Winner, Older 1986

Big Bushy Mustache by Gary Soto. Joe Cepeda, ill. Knopf, 1998. 3.1/K-3
To look like his father in the Cinco de Mayo play, Ricky borrows a mustache from a school costume and loses it, but his father comes up with a replacement.
Américas Commended 1998

The Big Idea by Ellen Schecter. Bob Dorsey, ill. Hyperion, 1996. 3.5/3-6
Luz is determined to turn a run-down vacant lot into a garden like the one her grandmother had in Puerto Rico and must convince her neighbors to help.
Américas Commended 1996

Big Moon Tortilla by Joy Cowley. Dyanne Strongbow, ill. Boyds Mills, 1998. 3.8/3-6
Marta has a bad day at the Tohono O'Odham reservation in Arizona after the dog eats her homework and she breaks her glasses, but Grandmother helps her feel better.
Américas Commended 1998

Billy by Laura Roybal. Houghton Mifflin, 1994. oop. na/7-10
Billy, a sixteen-year-old boy who is reunited with the family he was kidnapped from by his natural father six years earlier, tries to sort out his identity.
Américas Commended 1994

Birdland by Tracy Mack. Scholastic, 2003. 7.0/7-12
A fourteen-year-old, tongue-tied boy spends Christmas break filming a documentary about his New York neighborhood and remembering his dead brother.
Sydney Taylor Honor, Older 2003

The Birthday Swap by Loretta López. Lee & Low, 1997. 2.0/K-3, 3.1/K-3
A Mexican-American girl who will not be six until December has a great deal to celebrate when her sister swaps birthdays with her.
Américas Commended 1997

Black Cat by Christopher Myers. Scholastic, 1999. 3.6/K-3
A black cat wanders through the streets of a city.
Coretta Scott King Honor, Illustrator 2000

Black Child by Peter Mugabane. Knopf, 1982. oop. na/ya
South African history.
Coretta Scott King Winner, Illustrator 1983

Black Dance in America: A History Through Its People by James Haskins. Crowell, 1990. oop. na/6-12
Black dance in America from its beginnings through tap and modern dance to break dancing.
Coretta Scott King Honor, Author 1991

Black Diamond: The Story of the Negro Baseball Leagues by Patricia C. McKissack and Fredrick L. McKissack. Scholastic, 1994. 7.7/5-8
History of baseball in the Negro Leagues and its heroes, including Monte Irwin, Buck Leonard, and Cool Papa Bell.
Coretta Scott King Honor, Author 1995

Black Hands, White Sails: The Story of African-American Whalers by Patricia C. McKissack and Fredrick L. McKissack. Scholastic, 1999. 8.0/3-6
African-American whalers between 1730 and 1880, their contributions to the industry, and their role in the abolitionist movement.
Carter G. Woodson Honor, Secondary 2000   Coretta Scott King Honor, Author 2000

Black Music in America: A History Through Its People by James Haskins. Harper and Row, 1987. oop. na/6-12
History of black music in America, from early slave songs through jazz and the blues to soul, classical music, and current trends.
Carter G. Woodson Winner 1988

Black Troubadour: Langston Hughes by Charlemae Rollins. Rand McNally, 1970. oop. na/7-12
Biography of the famous twentieth-century African-American poet.
Coretta Scott King Winner, Author 1971

La Boda: A Mexican Wedding Celebration by Nancy Van Laan. Andrea Arroyo, ill. Little, Brown, 1996. oop. na/K-3
A girl and her grandmother watch village members participate in a traditional Zapotec Indian wedding celebration.
Américas Commended 1996

Born Confused by Tanuja Desai Hidier. Scholastic, 2002. 5.9/7-12, 8.0/7-12
Dimple, whose family is from India, discovers that she is not Indian enough for Indians and not American enough for Americans.
Asian Pacific American Honor, Text 2004

The Bossy Gallito: A Traditional Cuban Folk Tale/El gallo de bodas by Lucía M. González. Lulu Delacre ill. Scholastic, 1994. 2.0/K-3, 3.4/K-3
Cumulative Cuban folktale in which a rooster dirties his beak on a kernel of corn and must clean it before his parrot uncle's wedding.
Américas Commended 1994   Pura Belpré Honor, Illustration and Narrative 1996

Breaking Ground, Breaking Silence: The Story of New York's African Burial Ground by Joyce Hansen and Gary McGowan. Henry Holt, 1998. 6.0/5-8
Discovery and study of an African burial site found in Manhattan in 1991 and what it reveals about the lives of black people in Colonial times.
Coretta Scott King Honor, Author 1999

Breaking the Chains: African-American Slave Resistance by William Katz. Atheneum, 1990. 8.8/5-8
Slavery in the United States, harsh conditions, resistance, revolts, and the involvement of slaves in the Civil War.
Carter G. Woodson Outstanding Merit, Secondary 1991

Breaking Through by Francisco Jiménez. Houghton Mifflin, 2001. 5.3/7-12
Having come from Mexico to California ten years ago, Francisco is fighting to improve his life and complete his education.
Américas Winner 2001   Pura Belpré Honor, Narrative 2002
Tomás Rivera Winner 2001

Bright Shadow by Joyce Carol Thomas. Avon, 1983. 7.0/7-12
Abyssinia must cope with tragedy when peace is shattered in her Oklahoma countryside and her boyfriend disappears.
Coretta Scott King Honor, Author 1984

Bronx Masquerade by Nikki Grimes. Dial, 2002. 4.5/7-12
While studying the Harlem Renaissance, students at a Bronx high school read poems they've written, revealing their innermost thoughts and fears to their classmates.
Coretta Scott King Winner, Author 2003

Brothers: A Hebrew Legend by Florence B. Freedman. Robert Andrew Parker, ill. Harper & Row, 1985. oop. 2.5/K-3
Hard times on adjoining farms bring about acts of kindness and a celebration of brothers living in friendship.
Sydney Taylor Winner, Younger 1985

Brown Honey in Broomwheat Tea: Poems by Joyce Carol Thomas. Floyd Cooper, ill. HarperCollins, 1993. 4.0/3-6
Poems exploring African-American identity.
Coretta Scott King Honor, Author 1994   Coretta Scott King Honor, Illustrator 1994

Bubby, Me, and Memories by Barbara Pomerantz. Leon Lurie, ill. UAHC, 1983. oop. na/K-3
Depicts the loss felt by a child after the death of her grandmother.
Sydney Taylor Winner, Older 1983

Bud, Not Buddy by Christopher Paul Curtis. Delacorte, 1999. 4.0/3-6, 5.0/5-8
Bud, a motherless boy during the Great Depression, escapes a foster home and sets out in search of his father.
Coretta Scott King Winner, Author 2000

Buffalo Days by Diane Hoyt-Goldsmith. Lawrence Migdale, ill. Holiday House, 1997. 5.8/3-6
Life on a Crow Indian reservation in Montana and the importance the tribe places on buffalo, once again thriving in areas where the Crow live.
Carter G. Woodson Honor, Elementary 1998

Buffalo Hunt by Russell Freedman. Holiday House, 1988. 6.4/3-6
Buffalo in the lore and day-to-day life of the Indian tribes of the Great Plains.
Carter G. Woodson Outstanding Merit, Elementary 1989

Buried Onions by Gary Soto. Harcourt, 1997, 1999. 7.0/7-12, 8.0/7-12
Eddie drops out of college and struggles to find a place as a Mexican American in a violence-infested neighborhood of Fresno, California.
Américas Commended 1997

Butterfly Boy by Virginia Kroll. Gerardo Suzán, ill. Boyds Mills, 1997. 2.0/K-3
A boy and grandfather watch a gathering of butterflies in Mexico.
Américas Commended 1997

C.L.O.U.D.S by Pat Cummings. Lothrop, Lee & Shepard, 1986. oop. na/K-3
Chuku the angel is given the job of painting the skies of New York City.
Coretta Scott King Honor, Illustrator 1987

Cakes and Miracles: A Purim Tale by Barbara Diamond Goldin. Erika Weihs, ill. Viking, 1991. Puffin, 1993. oop. 3.0/K-3
Young, blind Hershel finds that he has special gifts he can use to help his mother during the Jewish holiday of Purim.
Sydney Taylor Winner, Younger 1991

Call Me Ruth by Marilyn Sachs. Doubleday, 1982. Beech Tree, 1995. oop. 5.1/3-6
Daughter of a Russian immigrant family in 1908 Manhattan has conflicting feelings about her mother's increasingly radical union involvement.
Sydney Taylor Winner 1982

Calling the Doves/El canto de las palomas by Juan Felipe Herrera. Elly Simmons, ill. Children's Book Press, 1995. 4.5/3-6
Author recalls his childhood in California with his farmworker parents who inspired him with poetry and song.
Américas Commended 1995

Canto Familiar by Gary Soto. Annika Nelson, ill. Harcourt, 1995. 4.0/3-6
Poems about the pleasures and woes of Mexican-American children growing up.
Américas Commended 1995

The Captive by Joyce Hansen. Scholastic, 1994. oop. 5.1/3-6
When Kofi is sold as a slave and ends up in Massachusetts, his fate is in the hands of Paul Cuffe, African-American shipbuilder who works to return slaves to Africa.
Coretta Scott King Honor, Author 1995

Caribbean Alphabet by Frane Lessac. Morrow, 1994. oop. na/K-3
Alphabet of images from the Caribbean including hibiscus, mangoes, and reggae.
Américas Commended 1994

A Caribbean Counting Book compiled by Faustin Charles. Roberta Arenson, ill. Houghton Mifflin, 1996. 2.0/K-3
Rhymes that are chanted as songs and in games in Caribbean countries.
Américas Commended 1996

A Caribbean Dozen: Poems from Caribbean Poets edited by John Agard and Grace Nichols. Cathie Felstead, ill. Candlewick, 1994. oop. na/3-6
Thirteen Caribbean poets recount childhood experiences.
Américas Commended 1995

Caribbean Dream by Rachel Isadora. Putnam, 1998. 1.0/P-2
Lyrical and evocative dreamscape of the Caribbean.
Américas Commended 1998

Carlos and the Skunk/Carlos y el zorrillo by Jan Romero Stevens.
Jeanne Arnold, ill. Patricia Hinton Davison, trans. Rising Moon, 1997.
2.0/K-3
Carlos shows off for Gloria by catching a skunk but gets more than he
bargained for.
Américas Commended 1997

Carlos, Light the Farolito by Jean Ciavonne. Donna Clair, ill. Clarion,
1995. 2.0/K-3
When his parents and grandfather are late on Christmas Eve, Carlos
takes over his grandfather's role in the traditional reenactment of Las
Posadas.
Américas Commended 1995

Carnaval by George Ancona. Harcourt, 1999. 4.0/3-6, 5.3/3-6
Traditions and rituals of the celebration of Carnaval in Brazil.
Américas Commended 1999

Carter G. Woodson: The Father of Black History by Patricia C.
McKissack and Fredrick L. McKissack. Ned O., ill. Enslow, 1991,
2002. 3.0/3-6
Life and accomplishments of the man who pioneered the study of black
history.
Carter G. Woodson Outstanding Merit, Elementary 1992

Carter G. Woodson: The Man Who Put "Black" in American History
by James Haskins and Kathleen Benson. Melanie Reim, ill. Millbrook
Press, 2000. 7.3/4-6
Biography of the son of former slaves who received a Ph.D. in history
from Harvard and devoted his life to bringing the achievements of his
race to the world's attention.
Carter G. Woodson Honor, Middle Level 2001

Carver: A Life in Poems by Marilyn Nelson. Front Street, 2001. 5.9/7-12
George Washington Carver's life is evoked in lyrical poems.
Coretta Scott King Honor, Author 2002

The Castle on Hester Street by Linda Heller. Jewish Publication Society, 1982. oop. 2.5/K-3
Julie's grandmother deflates her husband's tall tales about their journey from Russia to America and their life on Hester Street.
Sydney Taylor Winner 1982

Celebrate! in Central America by Joe Viesti and Diane Hall. Joe Viesti, ill. Lothrop, Lee & Shepard, 1997. oop. na/3-6
Background and customs associated with Central American festivals.
Américas Commended 1997

Celebrating Chinese New Year by Diane Hoyt-Goldsmith. Lawrence Migdale, ill. Holiday House, 1998. 6.0/K-3, 6.0/1-6
A San Francisco boy and his family prepare for and celebrate Chinese New Year.
Carter G. Woodson Honor, Elementary 1999

Celebrating Hanukkah by Diane Hoyt-Goldsmith. Lawrence Migdale, ill. Holiday House, 1996. 4.0/3-6
History, traditions, and significance of Hanukkah as celebrated by a Jewish family in San Francisco.
Carter G. Woodson Honor, Elementary 1997

Celebrating Kwanzaa by Diane Hoyt-Goldsmith. Lawrence Migdale, ill. Holiday House, 1993. 4.0/3-6
A Chicago family celebrates the African-American holiday, Kwanzaa.
Carter G. Woodson Outstanding Merit, Elementary 1994

Celebrating the Hero by Lyll Becerra de Jenkins. Lodestar, 1993. oop. na/7-12
After her mother's death, Camila travels to Colombia to attend a ceremony honoring her late grandfather and learns some disturbing truths.
Américas Commended 1993

Cendrillon: A Caribbean Cinderella by Robert D. San Souci. Brian Pinkney, ill. Simon & Schuster, 1998. 3.0/3-6, 4.0/3-6
Creole variant of a Cinderella tale set in the Caribbean.
Américas Honorable Mention 1998

César Chávez: The Struggle for Justice/César Chávez: la lucha por la justicia by Richard Griswold del Castillo. Piñata Books, 2002. 2.0/K-3
Biography of Mexican-American labor leader of the United Farm Workers.
Carter G. Woodson Winner, Elementary 2003.

Chanukah on the Prairie by Burt E. Schuman. Rosalind Charney Kaye, ill. UAHC Press, 2002. 2.0/2-4
An immigrant family from Poland is welcomed by a Jewish community in North Dakota.
Sydney Taylor Honor, Younger 2003

The Chanukkah Guest by Eric Kimmel. Giora Carmi, ill. Holiday House, 1990. 3.0/K-3
On the first night of Chanukkah, Old Bear wanders into Bubba Brayna's house and receives a helping of potato latkes when she mistakes him for the rabbi.
Sydney Taylor Winner, Younger 1990

Chato and the Party Animals by Gary Soto. Susan Guevara, ill. Putnam, 2000. 3.0/K-3
Chato decides to throw a pachanga for his friend Novio Boy, who has never had a birthday party, but when it is time to party, Novio Boy cannot be found.
Pura Belpré Winner, Illustration 2002

Chato's Kitchen by Gary Soto. Susan Guevara, ill. Putnam, 1995. 2.0/K-3
To get the ratoncitos (mice) who have moved into the barrio to come to his house, Chato the cat prepares all kinds of good food: fajitas, frijoles, salsa, enchiladas, and more.
Américas Honorable Mention 1995   Pura Belpré Winner,
Illustration 1996   Tomás Rivera Winner 1995

Chave's Memories/Las recuerdos de Chave by María Isabel Delgado. Yvonne Symank, ill. Piñata Books, 1996. 2.0/K-3
Recollections of childhood visits to a ranch in Mexico, playing with cousins, and listening to the stories of the old Indian ranch hand.
Américas Commended 1996

Chicken Soup by Heart by Esther Hershenhorn. Rosanne Litzinger, ill. Simon & Schuster, 2002. 3.1/P-2
When Rudie's sitter gets the flu, he makes her a batch of special chicken soup that includes a secret ingredient—stories from the heart.
Sydney Taylor Winner, Younger 2002

Children of the Civil Rights Era by Catherine A. Welch. Carolrhoda Books, 2002. 4.9/3-6
Courageous young people who marched, protested, and risked their lives to end racial discrimination in the South in the 1950s and 1960s.
Carter G. Woodson Honor, Elementary 2002

Children of the Maya: A Guatemalan Indian Odyssey by Brent Ashabranner. Paul Conklin, ill. Dodd Mead, 1986. oop. na/6-8
Examines the plight of Mayans who fled the violent political situation in Guatemala and settled in Florida.
Carter G. Woodson Outstanding Merit 1987

Children of the Relocation Camps by Catherine A. Welch. Carolrhoda Books, 2000. 4.1/3-6
Experiences of Japanese-American children who were moved to relocation centers during World War II.
Carter G. Woodson Honor, Elementary 2001

Children of the Tlingit by Frank Staub. Carolrhoda Books, 1999. 5.8/3-6
History, geography, and culture of the Tlingit people in Southeast Alaska.
Carter G. Woodson Honor, Elementary 2000

The Children of Topaz: The Story of a Japanese-American Internment Camp Based on a Classroom Diary by Michael O. Tunnell and George W. Chilcoat. Holiday House, 1996. 7.6/3-6
Diary of a third-grade class of Japanese-American children being held with their families in an internment camp during World War II.
Carter G. Woodson Honor, Secondary 1997

Childtimes: A Three-Generation Memoir by Eloise Greenfield and Lessie Jones Little. Jerry Pinkney, ill. Harper, 1979. 5.0/4-6
Childhood memoirs of a black grandmother, mother, and daughter between the 1880s and the 1950s. Includes materials by Pattie Ridley Jones.
Coretta Scott King Honor, Author 1980

The Chinese Americans by Milton Meltzer. Crowell, 1980. oop. na/6-9
History of the Chinese in the United States, their contributions to the development of this country, and their struggle for economic and social equality.
Carter G. Woodson Winner 1981

The Christmas Gift/El regalo de Navidad by Francisco Jiménez. Claire B. Cotts, ill. Houghton Mifflin, 2000. 4.5/K-3
When his family has to move a few days before Christmas to find work, Panchito worries that he will not get the gift he wants.
Américas Commended 2000

Christmas in the Big House, Christmas in the Quarters by Patricia C. McKissack and Fredrick L. McKissack. Scholastic, 1994. 4.0/3-6
Customs, recipes, poems, and songs to celebrate Christmas in plantation houses and in the slave quarters before the Civil War.
Coretta Scott King Winner, Author 1995

Circle of Gold by Candy Dawson Boyd. Scholastic, 1984, 1994. 4.0/3-6
Mattie copes with the loss of her father and her mixed feelings toward her mother who must now support the family.
Coretta Scott King Honor, Author 1985

The Circuit: Stories from the Life of a Migrant Child by Francisco Jiménez. University of New Mexico Press, 1997. Houghton Mifflin, 1999. 5.3/5-8
Interconnected stories about Francisco, who has to move from school to school when his parents move to find work.
Américas Winner 1997

A Cloak for the Moon by Eric Kimmel. Katya Krenina, ill. Holiday House, 2001. oop. 3.6/K-3
A tailor who dreams that the moon is cold in the sky searches for a special fabric with which to make it a cloak.
Sydney Taylor Honor, Younger 2001

Cocoa Ice by Diana Appelbaum. Holly Meade, ill. Orchard, 1997. oop. 4.7/K-5
A girl in Santo Domingo tells how cocoa is harvested during the late 1800s and her counterpart in Maine tells about the harvesting of ice.
Américas Commended 1997

The Color of My Words by Lynn Joseph. HarperCollins, 2000. 4.0/3-6, 5.1/3-6
When life in the Dominican Republic gets difficult, Ana Rosa, a would-be writer, depends on her brother to make her feel better until the events on her thirteenth birthday.
Américas Winner 2000

Coming Home: A Story of Josh Gibson, Baseball's Greatest Home Run Hitter by Nanette Mellage. Cornelius Van Wright, ill and Ying-Hwa Hu, ill. BridgeWater Books, 2001. oop. 4.2/1-4
Carter G. Woodson Winner, Elementary 2002

Coming to North America from Mexico, Cuba and Puerto Rico by Susan Carver and Paula McGuire. Delacorte, 1981. oop. na/6-9
Immigrant experiences of Mexicans, Cubans, and Puerto Ricans in the U.S.
Carter G. Woodson Winner 1982

The Composition by Antonio Skármeta. Alfonso Ruano, ill. Groundwood, 2000, 2003. 4.0/3-6
When a government official tells students to write a composition, Pedro must decide how he feels about the dictatorship in his country.
Américas Winner 2000

Confetti: Poems for Children by Pat Mora. Enrique O. Sánchez, ill. Lee & Low, 1996. 2.0/K-3
Poems celebrating the beauty of the Southwest as experienced by a Mexican-American girl.
Américas Commended 1996

Cool Melons—Turn to Frogs! The Life and Poems of Issa story and translations by Matthew Gollub. Kazuko G. Stone, ill. Calligraphy by Keiko Smith. Lee & Low, 1998. 4.4/K-3
Biography and introduction to a Japanese haiku poet whose love for nature found expression in his poems.
Asian Pacific American Honor 2000

Cool Salsa: Bilingual Poems on Growing Up Latino in the United States edited by Lori M. Carlson. Henry Holt, 1994. 7.0/7-12
Collection of poems by U. S. Latino writers.
Américas Commended 1994

Coolies by Yin. Chris Soentpiet, ill. Philomel, 2001. 4.8/3-6
A boy hears the story of his great-great-great-grandfather and brother who came to the U.S. to make a better life while helping to build the transcontinental railroad.
Asian Pacific American Honor, Illustration 2004

Coretta Scott King by Lillie Patterson. Garrard, 1977. oop. na/3-6
Biography of the widow of slain civil rights leader, Martin Luther King, Jr.
Coretta Scott King Honor, Author 1978

Cornrows by Camille Yarbrough. Carole Byard, ill. Coward-McCann, 1979. oop. 3.8/3-6
Explains how the hair style of cornrows, a symbol in Africa since ancient times, now symbolizes the courage of outstanding Afro-Americans.
Coretta Scott King Winner, Illustrator 1980

Count on Your Fingers African Style by Claudia Zaslavsky. Jerry Pinkney, ill. Crowell, 1980. 4.0/3-6
Describes how finger counting is used to communicate price and quantity in an East African market place.
Coretta Scott King Honor, Illustrator 1981

The Crab Man by Patricia E. Van West. Cedric Lucas, ill. Miguel Arisa, trans. Turtle Books, 1998. 2.0/K-3
When Neville sees the crabs he collected being mistreated by the man at a Jamaican hotel, he no longer wants to supply them but would thereby forfeit his income.
Américas Commended 1998

CrashBoomLove: A Novel in Verse by Juan Felipe Herrera. University of New Mexico Press, 1999. 3.6/7-12
After his father leaves, Cesar lives with his mother and struggles through painful experiences of growing up as a Mexican-American high school student.
Américas Winner 1999

The Creation by James Weldon Johnson. James Ransome, ill. Holiday House, 1994. 4.1/K-3
Poem based on the story of creation from the Bible.
Coretta Scott King Winner, Illustrator 1995

A Cry from the Earth: Music of the North American Indians by John Bierhorst. Four Winds Press, 1979. oop. na/9-12
Overview of American Indian music and dance, instruments, structure, and the importance of music in Indian life.
Carter G. Woodson Outstanding Merit 1980

Cuba: After the Revolution by Bernard Wolf. Dutton, 1999. oop. 7.3/4-6
Daily life of Ana, daughter of two Havana artists, as she goes to
school, takes ballet lessons, and plays in the park.
Américas Honorable Mention 1999

Cuba 15 by Nancy Osa. Delacorte, 2003. 8-0/7-12
Violet, a Chicago high school student, reluctantly prepares for her
upcoming quince, celebration of a Latina's fifteenth birthday.
Américas Honorable Mention 2003   Pura Belpré Honor,
Narrative 2004

Cuban Kids by George Ancona. Marshall Cavendish, 2000. 3.0/3-6
Photographs of children in Cuba.
Américas Commended 2000

*La Cucaracha Martina: A Caribbean Folktale/La Cucaracha Martina:
Un Cuento Folklórico del Caribe* by Daniel Moretón. Turtle, 1997.
2.0/K-3
While searching for the source of a beautiful sound, a ravishing
cockroach rejects marriage proposals from a menagerie of city animals
that woo her with noises.
Américas Commended 1997

Cuckoo/Cucu by Lois Ehlert. Gloria de Aragón Andújar, trans.
Harcourt Brace, 1997. 2.0/K-3
Traditional Mayan tale that reveals how the cuckoo lost her beautiful
feathers.
Américas Commended 1997

Daddy's Chair by Sandy Lanton. Shelly O. Haas, ill. Kar-Ben Copies,
1991. Lanton Haas Press, 2001. 2.0/K-3
When Michael's father dies, his family sits shiva, observes the Jewish
week of mourning, and remembers the good things about him.
Sydney Taylor Winner, Younger 1991

Dancing on the Bridge of Avignon by Ida Vos. Terese Edelstein, trans. and Inez Smidt, trans. Houghton Mifflin, 1995. 8.0/7-12
Experiences of a Jewish girl and her family during Nazi occupation of the Netherlands.
Sydney Taylor Winner, Older 1995

Daniel Inouye by Jane Goodsell. Haru Wells, ill. Crowell, 1977. oop. na/3-6
Biography of the first Congressman from Hawaii and the first American of Japanese descent to serve in the U. S. Congress.
Carter G. Woodson Winner 1978

The Daring Escape of Ellen Craft by Cathy Moore. Mary O'Keefe Young, ill. Carolrhoda Books, 2002. 3.2/3-6
Biographical account of a fugitive slave couple's escape in 1848.
Carter G. Woodson Honor, Elementary 2003

Dark Harvest: Migrant Farmworkers in America by Brent Ashabranner. Paul Conklin, ill. Dodd, Mead, 1985. Linnet, 1993. 7.1/7-12
An account of farmworkers' lives.
Carter G. Woodson Winner 1986

The Dark-Thirty: Southern Tales of the Supernatural by Patricia C. McKissack. Knopf, 1992. 4.6/4-8
Ghost stories with African-American themes designed to be told during the half hour before sunset when ghosts seem all too believable.
Coretta Scott King Winner, Author 1993

Darkfright by Holly Young Huth. Jenny Stow, ill. Atheneum, 1996. oop. na/K-3
Despite her neighbors, a woman who is afraid of the dark stays awake all night and sleeps during the day until a broken star helps her see things differently.
Américas Commended 1996

Day of the Dead by Tony Johnson and Jeanette Winter. Harcourt Brace, 1997. 2.0/K-3
A Mexican family prepares for and celebrates the Day of the Dead.
Américas Commended 1997

Daydreamers by Eloise Greenfield. Tom Feelings, ill. Dial, 1981.
4.0/K-3
Depicts the world of daydreamers.
Coretta Scott King Honor, Illustrator 1982

Days of Jubilee: The End of Slavery in the United States by Patricia C.
McKissack and Fredrick L. McKissack. Scholastic, 2003. 8.2/3-6
Slave narratives, letters, diaries, military orders, and other documents
chronicle the stages leading to the emancipation of slaves.
Coretta Scott King Honor, Author 2004

*The Days When the Animals Talked: Black Folk Tales and How They
Came to Be* by William J. Faulkner. Troy Howell, ill. Follett, 1977.
Africa World Press, 1993. 4.0/3-6
Afro-American folktales featuring the escapades of Brer Rabbit and
tales describing the lives of Afro-American slaves.
Coretta Scott King Honor, Author 1978

De Colores and Other Latin American Folk Songs for Children by
Jose-Luis Orozco. Elisa Kleven, ill. Dutton, 1994. 2.0/K-3, 4.0/3-6
Collection of folk songs from Latin American countries.
Américas Commended 1994

Dear Abuelita/Querida Abuela by Sofía Meza Keane. Enrique O.
Sánchez, ill. Rigby, 1997. oop. na/K-3
Letters to a Latina grandmother.
Américas Commended 1997

Dear Benjamin Banneker by Andrea Davis Pinkney. Brian Pinkney, ill.
Harcourt, 1994. 4.0/3-6, 6.4/3-6
Biography of a scientist, thinker, and farmer born in 1731.
Carter G. Woodson Outstanding Merit, Elementary 1995

The Devil in Vienna by Doris Orgel. Dial, 1978. Puffin, 1988. 4.4/5-8,
6.3/5-8
A Jewish girl and the daughter of a Nazi have been friends since they
started school, but in 1938 they find their relationship difficult to
maintain.
Sydney Taylor Winner 1978

The Devil's Arithmetic by Jane Yolen. Viking, 1988. Puffin, 1990. 4.6/5-8, 6.0/5-8
Hannah resents stories of her Jewish heritage and of the past until she finds herself in World War II Poland in a concentration camp.
Sydney Taylor Winner, Older 1988

The Diamond Tree: Jewish Tales from Around the World by Howard Schwartz and Barbara Rush. Uri Shulevitz, ill. HarperCollins, 1991. oop. 6.1/3-6
Jewish traditional nursery tales from many countries.
Sydney Taylor Honor, Older 1991

Diez Deditos/Ten Little Fingers and Other Play Rhymes and Action Songs from Latin America selected by Jose-Luis Orozco. Elisa Kleven, ill. Dutton, 1997. 2.0/K-3
Songs and games.
Américas Commended 1997

Doctor Bird: Three Lookin' Up Tales from Jamaica by Gerald Hausman and Ashley Wolff. Philomel, 1998. oop. 4.0/3-6
Stories featuring Doctor Bird, the clever hummingbird found only in Jamaica.
Américas Commended 1998

Don't Explain: A Song of Billie Holiday by Alexis De Veaux. Harper, 1980. oop. na/ya
Prose poem recounting the life of the American jazz singer known as Lady Day.
Coretta Scott King Honor, Author 1981

Down by the River: Afro-Caribbean Rhymes, Games and Songs for Children compiled by Grace Hallworth. Caroline Binch, ill. Scholastic, 1996. oop. na/K-3
Rhymes, chants, and games of Afro-Caribbean origin.
Américas Honorable Mention 1996

Dragonwings by Laurence Yep. Crowell, 1975. Cornerstone, 1990. 5.3/5-8, 6.0/5-8
In the early twentieth century a Chinese boy joins his father in San Francisco and helps him realize a dream, making a flying machine.
Carter G. Woodson Winner 1976

Duey's Tale by Pearl Bailey. Harcourt, 1975. oop. na/K-3
A maple seedling is separated from his mother tree, makes friends with a bottle and a log, and searches for his own place in life.
Coretta Scott King Winner, Author 1976

Duke Ellington: The Piano Prince and His Orchestra by Andrea Davis Pinkney. Brian Pinkney, ill. Hyperion, 1998. 3.0/3-6
Career of the jazz musician and composer who created music that was beyond category.
Coretta Scott King Honor, Illustrator 1999

Early Black Reformers edited by James Tackach. Greenhaven Press, 2003. 8.0/7-12, 9.0/7-12
African Americans who worked to improve social and political conditions in the U.S.
Carter G. Woodson Winner, Secondary 2004

Edmonia Lewis: Wildfire in Marble by Rinna Evelyn Wolfe. Dillon, 1998. oop. na/6-10
Biography of the first African/Chippewa woman to achieve fame as a sculptor.
Carter G. Woodson Winner, Secondary 1999

Elena by Diane Stanley. Hyperion, 1996. oop. na/3-5
A Mexican-American girl recounts how her mother moved the family to the U.S. during the Mexican Revolution.
Américas Commended 1996

Ella Fitzgerald: First Lady of Song by Katherine Krohn. Lerner, 2001. 6.9/7-12
Biography of the celebrated jazz singer known for her scat singing and recordings of the works of major American composers.
Carter G. Woodson Honor, Secondary 2002

An Enchanted Hair Tale by Alexis De Veaux. Cheryl Hanna, ill. Harper, 1987. oop. na/1–4
Sudan suffers from the ridicule of his strange-looking hair until he accepts and enjoys its enchantment.
Coretta Scott King Honor, Author 1988

The Endless Steppe: Growing Up in Siberia by Esther Hautzig. Crowell, 1968. G. K. Hall, 1973. Harper & Row, 1987. 6.3/7-12, 8.0/7-12
During World War II the author and her family were arrested by Russians and exiled to Siberia for five years.
Sydney Taylor Winner 1968

Erandi's Braids by Antonio Hernández Madrigal. Tomie De Paola, ill. Putnam, 1999. 3.5/K-3, 4.5/K-3
In a poor Mexican village Erandi offers to sell her long, beautiful hair to raise money to buy a fishing net.
Américas Commended 1999

Escape to Freedom: A Play about Young Frederick Douglass by Ossie Davis. Viking, 1976, Puffin, 1990. 6.0/5-8
Born a slave, Frederick Douglass endured years of cruelty before escaping to the North to claim his freedom.
Coretta Scott King Winner, Author 1979

Esperanza Rising by Pam Muñoz Ryan. Scholastic, 2000. 4.0/3-6, 5.3/5-8
Esperanza and her mother leave a life of wealth and privilege in Mexico to work in the labor camps of Southern California on the eve of the Great Depression.
Américas Honorable Mention 2000   Pura Belpré Winner, Narrative 2002

Everett Anderson's Goodbye by Lucille Clifton. Ann Grifalconi, ill. Holt, Rinehart & Winston, 1983. 2.0/K-3, 3.0/K-3
Everett has a difficult time coming to terms with grief after his father dies.
Coretta Scott King Winner, Author 1984

Exit from Home by Anita Heyman. Crown, 1977. oop. na/ya
A Jewish youth training to become a rabbi in turn-of-the-century
Russia is exposed to worldly ideas which change his attitude towards
his religion and country.
Sydney Taylor Winner 1977

The Face at the Window by Regina Hanson. Linda Saport, ill. Clarion,
1997. 3.4/3-6
When Dora goes to pick a mango from Miss Nella's tree, she is
frightened by the woman's strange behavior.
Américas Winner 1997

The Faithful Friend by Robert D. San Souci. Brian Pinkney, ill. Simon
& Schuster, 1995. 2.0/K-3, 5.2/3-6
Traditional tale from the French West Indies in which two friends,
Clement and Hippolyte, encounter love, zombies, and danger on the
island of Martinique.
Américas Commended 1995   Coretta Scott King Honor,
Illustrator 1996

Fallen Angels by Walter Dean Myers. Scholastic, 1988, Holt Rinehart
& Winston, 1988. 4.2/7-12
 Richie, just out of his Harlem high school, enlists in the Army in 1967
and spends a devastating year on active duty in Vietnam.
Coretta Scott King Winner, Author 1989

Family Pictures/Cuadros de familia by Carmen Lomas Garza.
Children's Book Press, 1990. 2.0/K-3, 4.3/3-6
Experiences of a Mexican-American artist growing up in Texas.
Pura Belpré Honor, Illustration 1996

The Farolitos of Christmas by Rudolfo Anaya. Edward Gonzáles, ill.
Hyperion, 1995. 2.0/K-3
With her father fighting in World War II and her grandfather too sick
to create traditional luminarias, Luz helps create little lanterns for their
Christmas celebration.
Américas Commended 1995   Tomás Rivera Winner 1995

Feliz Nochebuena, Feliz Navidad: Christmas Feasts of the Hispanic Caribbean by Maricel E. Presilla. Ismael Espinosa Ferrer, ill. Henry Holt, 1994. oop. na/3-6
Christmas celebrations in the Caribbean.
Américas Commended 1994

A Fence Away from Freedom: Japanese Americans and World War II by Ellen Levine. Putnam's Sons, 1995. oop. na/7-12
Personal narratives about the treatment of the Japanese Americans during World War II.
Carter G. Woodson Winner, Secondary 1996

Fernando's Gift/El Regalo de Fernando by Douglas Keiser. Sierra Club, 1995. 2.0/K-3
Fernando, who lives in the rain forest of Costa Rica with his family, goes with his friend to look for her favorite climbing tree only to find it cut down.
Américas Commended 1995

Fiesta Fireworks by George Ancona. Lothrop, Lee & Shepard, 1998. oop. na/K-6
Describes the preparation of fireworks and the festival honoring San Juan de Dios, the patron saint of Tultepec, Mexico, famed for its master pyrotechnics.
Américas Commended 1998

Fiesta U.S.A. by George Ancona. Osvaldo J. Blanco, trans. Dutton, 1995. 3.0/3-6
An introduction to the celebrations of Day of the Dead, Las Posadas, Los Matachines, and La Fiesta de los Reyes Magos (Three Kings).
Américas Commended 1995

Fireflies in the Dark: The Story of Friedl Dicker-Brandeis and the Children of Terezin by Susan Goldman Rubin. Holiday House, 2000. 6.2/5-8
Friedl Dicker, a Jewish woman from Czechoslovakia, taught art to children at the Terezin Concentration Camp.
Sydney Taylor Honor, Older 2000

Firefly Summer by Pura Belpré. Piñata Books, 1996. 6.0/5-8
At a plantation in rural Puerto Rico around the turn of the century, the foreman pursues a mystery surrounding his family.
Américas Commended 1996

First Day in Grapes by L. King Pérez. Robert Casilla, ill. Lee & Low, 2002. 3.2/K-3
When Chico starts the third grade after his family moves to begin harvesting California grapes, he finds that confidence and math skills help him cope.
Pura Belpré Honor, Illustration 2004

The First Part Last by Angela Johnson. Simon & Schuster Books, 2003. 4.7/7-12, 8.0/7-12
Bobby's carefree teenage life changes when he becomes a father and must care for his baby daughter.
Coretta Scott King Winner, Author 2004

The Flight of Red Bird: The Life of Zitkala-Sa by Doreen Rappaport. Dial, 1997. 7.1/5-8
Chronicles through reminiscences, letters, speeches, and stories, the experiences of a Yankton Indian woman's life in the nineteenth and early twentieth centuries.
Carter G. Woodson Honor, Elementary 1998

Flight to Freedom by Ana Veciana-Suarez. Orchard, 2002. 5.6/5-8, 8.0/7-12
Writing in a diary, Yara describes life with her family in Cuba in 1967 and her experiences in Florida after immigrating there.
Américas Commended 2002

For the Life of Laetitia by Merle Hodge. Farrar, Straus & Giroux, 1993. 5.2/7-12
As the first in her family to go to secondary school, Lacey struggles with problems including a cruel teacher and a difficult home life.
Américas Commended 1993

Forged by Fire by Sharon M. Draper. Atheneum, 1997. 6.0/7-12, 8.0/7-12

Gerald, who has spent years protecting his fragile half-sister from their abusive father, faces the prospect of one final confrontation.

Coretta Scott King Winner, Author 1998

Francie by Karen English. Farrar, Straus & Giroux, 1999. 4.0/3-6, 4.2/5-8, 6.0/5-8

When the boy whom she tutors in reading is accused of attempting to murder a white man, Francie gets in serious trouble.

Coretta Scott King Honor, Author 2000

Freedom River by Doreen Rappaport. Bryan Collier, ill. Hyperion, 2000. 3.1/K-3, 3.3/K-3

An incident in the life of John Parker, an ex-slave who became a businessman in Ohio and risked his life to help other slaves escape to freedom.

Coretta Scott King Honor, Illustrator 2001

Frida by Jonah Winter. Ana Juan, ill. Scholastic, 2002. 1.0/P-2, 2.5/P-2

Mexican artist Frida Kahlo lived a life filled with challenges.

Américas Honorable Mention 2002

The Friendship by Mildred D. Taylor. Max Ginsburg, ill. Dial, 1987. 4.1/3-6

Four children witness a confrontation between an elderly black man and a white storekeeper in rural Mississippi in the 1930s.

Coretta Scott King Winner, Author 1988

From Father to Son/De Padre a Hijo by Patricia Almada. Marianno de López, ill. Rigby, 1997. oop. na/K-3

The family baking tradition is passed from father to son.

Américas Commended 1997

From the Bellybutton of the Moon and Other Summer Poems/Del Ombligo de la Luna y otros poemas de verano by Francisco X. Alarcón. Maya Christina González, ill. Children's Book Press, 1998. 3.0/3-6
Bilingual poems celebrating childhood memories of summers, Mexico, and nature.
Américas Commended 1998   Pura Belpré Honor, Narrative 2000

From the Notebooks of Melanin Sun by Jacqueline Woodson. Scholastic, 1995. 7.0/7-12
Melanin's comfortable, quiet life is shattered when his mother reveals she has fallen in love with a woman.
Coretta Scott King Honor, Author 1996

Fruits: A Caribbean Counting Poem by Valerie Bloom. David Axtell, ill. Henry Holt, 1997. oop. na/K-3
Counting poem using Caribbean fruit including guavas, jackfruit, and Otaheiti apples.
Américas Honorable Mention 1997

The Garden of Happiness by Erika Tamar. Barbara Lambase, ill. Harcourt, 1996. 2.0/K-3
Marisol and her neighbors turn a vacant New York City lot into a lush community garden.
Américas Commended 1996

Gathering the Sun: An ABC in Spanish and English by Alma Flor Ada. Simón Silva, ill. Rosa Zubizarreta, trans. Lothrop, 1997. 5.2/K-3
Poems about working in the fields and nature's bounty, one for each letter of the Spanish alphabet.
Américas Commended 1997   Pura Belpré Honor, Illustration 1998

Gershon's Monster: A Story for the Jewish New Year by Eric Kimmel. Jon J. Muth, ill. Scholastic, 2000. 3.6/K-3
When his sins threaten the lives of his beloved twin children, a Jewish man repents of his wicked ways.
Sydney Taylor Winner, Younger 2000

A Gift for Abuelita: Celebrating the Day of the Dead/Un Regalo para Abuelita: En Celebración del Día de los Muertos by Nancy Luenn. Robert Chapman, ill. Rising Moon, 1998. 3.3/K-3, 3.3/2-5
After her grandmother dies, Rosita hopes to be reunited with Abuelita as she prepares a gift to give her when her family celebrates the Day of the Dead.
Américas Commended 1998

Goin' Someplace Special by Patricia C. McKissack. Jerry Pinkney, ill. Atheneum, 2001. 4.3/K-3
In segregated 1950s Nashville, an African-American girl braves indignities and obstacles to go to one of the few integrated places in town, the public library.
Coretta Scott King Winner, Illustrator 2002

Going Home by Eve Bunting. David Díaz, ill. HarperCollins, 1996. 2.0/K-3, 2.7/K-3
A Mexican family comes to the U. S. to work as farm laborers so their children will have opportunities, but the parents still consider Mexico their home.
Américas Commended 1996

The Golden Flower: A Taino Myth from Puerto Rico by Nina Jaffe. Enrique O. Sánchez, ill. Simon & Schuster, 1996. oop. na/K-3
Myth explaining the origin of the sea, the forest, and the island now called Puerto Rico.
Américas Commended 1996   Pura Belpré Honor, Illustration 1998

Golden Tales: Myths, Legends, and Folktales from Latin America/De Oro y Esmeraldas: Mitos, Leyendas y Cuentos Populares de Latino America by Lulu Delacre. Scholastic, 1996. 4.0/3-6
Latin American folktales.
Américas Commended 1996

Good News! by Sarita Chávez Silverman. Melinda Levine, ill.
Hampton-Brown, 1996. oop. na/K-3
Chago writes to his grandmother in the Dominican Republic about the
loss of his first tooth.
Américas Commended 1996.

Grandma and Me at the Flea/Los meros meros remateros by Juan
Felipe Herrera. Anita DeLucio-Brock, ill. Children's Book Press, 2002.
2.0/K-3
Juanito accompanies his grandmother to a flea market in southern
California, where they enjoy seeing old friends from their Mexican-
American community.
Américas Commended 2002

Grandmama's Joy by Eloise Greenfield. Carole Byard, ill. Collins,
1980. 2.0/K-3
A girl tries to cheer up her despondent grandmother by reminding her
of some very important things.
Coretta Scott King Honor, Illustrator 1981

Grandmother's Nursery Rhymes/Las nanas de Abuelita by Nelly
Palacio Jaramillo. Elivia Savadier, ill. Henry Holt, 1994. 2.0/K-3
Traditional South American nursery rhymes in Spanish and English.
Américas Commended 1994

Grannie Jus' Come! by Ana Sisnett. Karen Lusebrink, ill. Children's
Book Press, 1997. oop. na/K-3
Using Caribbean English a girl describes a visit from her grandmother
who arrives by bus and looks great in her new shoes and colorful
clothes.
Américas Commended 1997

The Great Migration: An American Story by Jacob Lawrence. Museum
of Modern Art, Phillips Collection, HarperCollins, 1993. 5.0/3-6
Paintings chronicle the journey of African Americans who, like the
artist's family, left the rural South in the early twentieth century to find
a better life in the industrial North.
Carter G. Woodson Outstanding Merit, Elementary 1994

Greetings, Sun by Phillis Gershator and David Gershator. Synthia Saint James, ill. DK Ink, 1998. 1.6/K-3
Throughout the day, children greet the sun, the breeze, their breakfasts, their school, and all the large and small sights they encounter.
Américas Commended 1998

The Gullywasher by Joyce Rossi. Northland Publishing, 1995. 3.0/3-6
Leticia's grandfather, a vaquero as a young man, provides fanciful explanations for how he got his wrinkles, white hair, round belly, and stooped frame.
Américas Commended 1995

Gwendolyn Brooks: Poet from Chicago by Martha E. Rhynes. Morgan Reynolds Publishing, 2003. 7.0/7-12.
Biography of an African-American poet, recipient of the National Book Award and Pulitzer Prize.
Carter G. Woodson Honor, Secondary 2004

Half a Moon and One Whole Star by Crescent Dragonwagon. Jerry Pinkney, ill. Macmillan, 1986. Aladdin Books, 1990. 4.2/K-3
The summer night is full of wonderful sounds and scents as Susan falls asleep.
Coretta Scott King Winner, Illustrator 1987

Hana's Suitcase: A True Story by Karen Levine. Second Story Press, 2002. A.Whitman, 2003. 4.0/3-6, 6.0/5-8
Biography of a Czech girl who died in the Holocaust, told in alternating chapters with an account of how the curator of a Japanese Holocaust center learned about her life.
Sydney Taylor Winner, Older 2002

Happily May I Walk: American Indians and Alaskan Natives Today by Arlene B. Hirschfelder. Charles Scribner's Sons, 1986. na/3-6, na/ya
Everyday life, culture, and preservation of the traditions of America's native peoples, the Indians, Inuits, and Aleuts.
Carter G. Woodson Winner 1987

The Hardest Lesson: Personal Accounts of a School Desegregation Crisis by Pamela Bullar and Judith Stoia. Little, Brown, 1980. oop. na/ya
Describes how desegregation of Boston schools in the 1970s affected the lives of individual students and adults, chosen to represent a cross section of the community.
Carter G. Woodson Outstanding Merit 1981

Harlem: A Poem by Walter Dean Myers. Christopher Myers, ill. Scholastic, 1997. 3.6/5-8
Poem celebrating the people, sights, and sounds of Harlem.
Coretta Scott King Honor, Illustrator 1998

The Harlem Renaissance by James Haskins. Millbrook Press, 1996. na/6-10, na/9+
Chronicles the early twentieth-century artistic and intellectual revolution in black America.
Carter G. Woodson Winner 1997

Harriet: The Life and World of Harriet Beecher Stowe by Norma Johnston. Four Winds Press, 1994. Beech Tree, 1996. oop. na/ya
Biography of Harriet Beecher Stowe.
Carter G. Woodson Outstanding Merit, Secondary 1995

Harvest by George Ancona. Marshall Cavendish, 2001. 4.0/3-6
Photo-documentary on the lives and work of Mexican migrant workers in the fields.
Américas Commended 2001

Harvesting Hope: The Story of Cesar Chavez by Kathleen Krull. Yuyi Morales, ill. Harcourt, 2003. 5.6/3-6
Biography of César Chávez, from age ten to age thirty-eight when he led a peaceful protest against the miserable working conditions of California migrant workers.
Américas Honorable Mention 2003   Pura Belpré Honor, Illustration 2004   Carter G. Woodson Honor, Elementary 2004

Heart of a Jaguar by Marc Talbert. Simon & Schuster, 1995. 5.9/7-12
Balam, a Mayan boy struggling to achieve manhood, participates in fasts, prayers, and rituals to appease the gods and bring rain to his village.
Américas Honorable Mention 1995

Heaven by Angela Johnson. Simon & Schuster, 1998. Thorndike Press, 2000. 4.7/7-12
Marley's seemingly perfect life in the small town of Heaven is disrupted when she discovers that her father and mother are not her real parents.
Coretta Scott King Winner, Author 1999

Hector Lives in the United States Now: The Story of a Mexican-American Child by Joan Hewett. Richard Hewett, ill. Lippincott, 1990. oop. na/4-6
Documents day-to-day happenings and milestones in the life of a Mexican boy whose family seeks amnesty in the U.S. under the Immigration Reform and Control Act.
Carter G. Woodson Outstanding Merit, Elementary 1991

Her Stories: African American Folktales, Fairy Tales, and True Tales by Virginia Hamilton. Leo Dillon, ill and Diane Dillon, ill. Scholastic, 1995. 4.69/3-6
Nineteen African-American stories featuring women.
Coretta Scott King Winner, Author 1996   Coretta Scott King Honor, Illustrator 1996

Hi! by Ann Herbert Scott. Glo Coalson, ill. Philomel, 1994. oop. na/K-3
While waiting in line with her mother at the post office, Margarita greets the patrons who come in carrying different types of mail.
Américas Commended 1995

Hispanic Voters: A Voice in American Politics by Judith Harlan. Franklin Watts, 1988. oop. na/ya
Examines the impact the nation's fastest growing minority is making on American politics. Includes Cubans, Mexican Americans, and Puerto Ricans.
Carter G. Woodson Outstanding Merit, Secondary 1989

Hoang Anh: A Vietnamese-American Boy by Diane Hoyt-Goldsmith. Lawrence Migdale, ill. Holiday House, 1992. 5.8/3-8
A Vietnamese-American boy describes the daily activities of his family in California and the traditional culture and customs that shape their lives.
Carter G. Woodson Outstanding Merit, Elementary 1993

Hooray, a Piñata! by Elisa Kleven. Lidia Díaz, trans. Dutton, 1996. 2.0/K-3, 2.9/K-3
After she chooses a cute dog piñata for her birthday party, Clara pretends it is her pet and doesn't want it to get broken.
Américas Commended 1996

How Iwariwa the Cayman Learned to Share: A Yanomami Myth by George Crespo. Clarion, 1995. oop. na/K-3
Animals in the Amazon rainforest find a way to trick the cayman into sharing the fire he uses to cook his food.
Américas Commended 1995

How Music Came to the World: An Ancient Mexican Myth by Hal Ober. Carol Ober, ill. Houghton Mifflin, 1994. 2.0/K-3
Retelling of a Mexican legend about music.
Américas Commended 1994

How My Family Lives in America by Susan Kuklin. Bradbury, 1992. 2.0/K-3
African-, Asian-, and Hispanic-American children describe their families' cultural traditions.
Carter G. Woodson Outstanding Merit, Elementary 1993

How Night Came from the Sea: A Story from Brazil by Mary-Joan Gerson. Carla Golembe, ill. Little, Brown, 1994. oop. na/K-3
Adaptation of a Brazilian tale about night.
Américas Commended 1994

Hue Boy by Rita Phillips Mitchell. Caroline Binch, ill. Dial, 1993. 2.2/K-3
Everyone in Hue Boy's island village has suggestions on how to help him grow, but he learns to stand tall in a way all his own.
Américas Commended 1993

The Hummingbird's Gift by Stefan Czernecki and Timothy Rhodes. Juliana Reyes de Silva, ill and Juan Hilario Silva, ill. Hyperion, 1994. oop. na/K-3
When Consuelo saves the hummingbirds' lives, they show her how to save her family from the drought.
Américas Commended 1994

The Hunterman and the Crocodile: A West African Folktale by Baba Wagué Diakité. Scholastic, 1997. 4.0/K-3
Donso, a West African hunterman, learns the importance of living in harmony with nature and the necessity of placing humans among, not above, other living things.
Coretta Scott King Honor, Illustrator 1998

I Am of Two Places/Soy de Dos Lugares edited by Mary Carden and Mary Cappellini. Maya Christina González, ill. Rigby, 1997. oop. na/K-3
Poetry about the immigrant experience.
Américas Commended 1997

I Am Rosa Parks by Rosa Parks with James Haskins. Wil Clay, ill. Dial, 1997. 2.0/K-3, 3.3/K-3
The black woman whose acts of civil disobedience led to the 1956 Supreme Court order to desegregate buses in Montgomery, Alabama, explains what she did and why.
Carter G. Woodson Honor 1998

I Hadn't Meant to Tell You This by Jacqueline Woodson. Delacorte, 1994. 4.1/5-8
Marie, the only black girl in the eighth grade willing to befriend her white classmate, discovers that Lena's father is doing horrible things to her in private.
Coretta Scott King Honor, Author 1995

I Have a News: Rhymes from the Caribbean by Walter Jekyll and Neil Philip. Jacqueline Mair, ill. William Morrow, 1994. oop. na/K-3
Traditional verses from the Caribbean.
Américas Commended 1994

I Have a Sister—My Sister Is Deaf by Jeanne Whitehouse Peterson.
Deborah Ray, ill. Harper, 1977. 3.3/P-2
A girl describes how her deaf sister experiences everyday things.
Coretta Scott King Honor, Author 1979

I Have Heard of a Land by Joyce Carol Thomas. Floyd Cooper, ill.
HarperCollins, 1998. 3.1/K-3, 4.0/3-6
Joys and hardships of an African-American pioneer woman who staked
a claim for free land in the Oklahoma territory.
Coretta Scott King Honor, Illustrator 1999

I Love Saturdays y domingos by Alma Flor Ada. Elivia Savadier, ill.
Atheneum, 2002. 2.0/K-3
A girl enjoys similarities and differences between her English- and
Spanish-speaking grandparents.
Américas Commended 2002

I Never Had It Made: The Autobiography of Jackie Robinson, as told to
Alfred Duckett. Putnam, 1972. Ecco Press, 1995. 8.0/7-12
Autobiography of an African American who broke the color barrier in
major league baseball and devoted his life to achieving justice.
Coretta Scott King Winner, Author 1973

i see the rhythm by Toyomi Igus. Michele Wood, ill. Children's Book
Press, 1998. 5.1/3-6
Chronicles and captures poetically the history, mood, and movement of
African-American music.
Coretta Scott King Winner, Illustrator 1999

*I Thought My Soul Would Rise and Fly: The Diary of Patsy, a Freed
Girl* by Joyce Hansen. Scholastic, 1997. 5.0/5-8, 6.0/5-8
Patsy keeps a diary of the ripe but confusing time after the Civil War
brought freedom to slaves.
Coretta Scott King Honor, Author 1998

I'm Going to Sing: Black American Spirituals by Ashley Bryan.
Atheneum, 1974, 1982. oop. na/2-8
Familiar and lesser-known spirituals including "Walk Together
Children," "Little David Play on Your Harp," "I Got Shoes," and
others.
Coretta Scott King Honor, Illustrator 1983

I'm José and I'm Okay: Three Stories from Bolivia by Werner
Holzwarth. Laura McKenna, trans. Kane/Miller, 1999. oop. na/4-7
A scrappy orphan works hard at his uncle's tire repair shop and proves
himself at work and in a bicycle race.
Américas Commended 1999

Icy Watermelon/Sandía fría by Mary Sue Galindo. Pauline Rodríguez
Howard, ill. Piñata Books, 2000. 2.9/K-3
Three generations of a family gather to eat watermelon, and the
grandparents reminisce about how the sweet fruit brought them
together.
Américas Commended 2000

*Iguanas in the Snow and Other Winter Poems/Iguanas en la nieve y
otros poemas de invierno* by Francisco X. Alarcón. Maya Christina
González, ill. Children's Book Press, 2001. 2.0/K-3
Fourth in a series, the poems in this picture book celebrate winter.
Américas Commended 2001   Pura Belpré Honor, Narrative 2002

Ike and Mama and the Block Wedding by Carol Snyder. Charles
Robinson, ill. Coward, McCann & Geoghegan, 1979. oop. na/4-6
Rosie is getting married on Sunday but not without help from the
residents of East 136th Street.
Sydney Taylor Winner 1979

Ike and Mama and the Seven Surprises by Carol Snyder. Charles
Robinson, ill. Lothrop, Lee and Shepard, 1985. oop. na/4-6
Ike is skeptical when his mother promises he will have seven surprises
before his Bar Mitzvah because his father is hospitalized and a jobless
cousin is living with them.
Sydney Taylor Winner, Older 1985

Imagining Isabel by Omar S. Castañeda. Lodestar, 1994. oop. na/7-12
Isabel, a newly married girl in a Mayan village, is invited to join a
teacher training program and is thrown into the reality of contemporary
Guatemala.
Américas Commended 1994

In America's Shadow by Kimberly Komatsu and Kaleigh Komatsu.
Thomas George Books, 2001. na/3-6
Experiences of Japanese Americans during World War II.
Carter G. Woodson Winner, Middle Level 2004

In Daddy's Arms I Am Tall: African Americans Celebrating Fathers by
Alan Schroeder. Javaka Steptoe, ill. Lee & Low, 1997. 3.1/K-3
Poems celebrating African-American fathers.
Coretta Scott King Winner, Illustrator 1998

In My Family: Paintings and Stories/En mi familia: Cuadros y relatos
by Carmen Lomas Garza. Francisco X. Alarcón, trans. Children's Book
Press, 1996. 2.0/K-3
Author uses art to portray her experiences growing up in south Texas.
Américas Winner 1996   Pura Belpré Honor, Illustration 1998
Tomás Rivera Winner 1996

In Rosa's Mexico by Campbell Geeslin. Andrea Arroyo, ill. Knopf,
1996. oop. na/K-3
In encounters with a rooster, burro, and wolf, a Mexican girl is able to
magically make things better.
Américas Commended 1996

In the Days of the Vaqueros: America's First True Cowboys by Russell
Freedman. Clarion, 2001. 7.0/3-6, 7.0/4-8
Early-day cowboys.
Américas Honorable Mention 2001

In the Mouth of the Wolf by Rose Zar. Jewish Publication Society,
1983. 8.0/7-12
Author's experiences in wartime Poland and surviving the Holocaust by
passing as an Aryan.
Sydney Taylor Winner, Younger 1983

In the Time of the Drums by Kim L. Sigelson. Brian Pinkney, ill. Hyperion, 1999. 4.6/3-6
Mentu, an American-born slave boy, watches his grandmother lead an insurrection of Ibo people arriving from Africa on a slave ship.
Coretta Scott King Winner, Illustrator 2000

In Two Worlds: A Yup'ik Eskimo Family by Aylette Jenness and Alice Rivers. Ayless Jenness, ill. Houghton Mifflin, 1989. oop. na/5-8
Documents the life of a Yup'ik Eskimo family, residents of an Alaskan town on the coast of the Bering Sea, detailing changes of the last fifty years.
Carter G. Woodson Winner, Elementary 1990

Indio by Sherry Garland. Harcourt, 1995. 7.0/7-12
Ipa struggles to survive a brutal time of change as the Spanish begin the conquest of the native people along the Texas border.
Américas Commended 1995

Into a Strange Land: Unaccompanied Refugee Youth in America by Brent Ashabranner and Melissa Ashabranner. Dodd, Mead, 1987. oop. na/ya
Individual stories of young Southeast Asian refugees, their problems, hopes, and successes.
Carter G. Woodson Outstanding Merit 1988

The Invisible Hunters: A Legend from the Miskito Indians of Nicaragua/Los cazadores invisibles: Una leyenda de los indios miskitos de Nicaragua compiled by Harriet Rohmer. Joe Sam, ill. Children's Book Press, 1987. 4.0/3-6
Miskito Indian legend set in seventeenth-century Nicaragua illustrates the impact of the first European traders on traditional life.
Coretta Scott King Honor, Illustrator 1988

Isla by Arthur Dorros. Elisa Kleven, ill. Sandra Marulanda Dorros, trans. Dutton, 1995. 2.7/K-3, 3.0/K-3
A girl and her grandmother take an imaginary journey to the Caribbean island where her mother grew up and some of her family still lives.
Américas Commended 1995

Island in the Sun by Harry Belafonte and Lord Burgess. Alex Ayliffe, ill. Dial, 1999. oop. na/K-3
Illustrations accompany words to a song made popular by Belafonte, paying tribute to his island childhood.
Américas Commended 1999

An Island Like You: Stories of the Barrio by Judith Ortiz Cofer.
Orchard Books, 1995. Puffin, 1996. 5.4/7-12, 7.0/7-12
Twelve stories about young people caught between their Puerto Rican heritage and American surroundings.
Américas Honorable Mention 1995   Pura Belpré Winner, Narrative 1996

The Island on Bird Street by Uri Orlev. Houghton Mifflin, 1983. 4.0/3-6, 4.6/5-8
During World War II a Jewish boy is left in a ruined house in the Warsaw ghetto and must learn to survive in life-threatening conditions.
Sydney Taylor Winner, Older 1984

Issues in Racism by Mary E. Williams. Lucent, 2000. 4.0/3-6
Discusses racial profiling, police brutality, stereotyping, white privilege, and the need for dialogue.
Carter G. Woodson Honor, Secondary 2001

It Doesn't Have to Be This Way/No tiene que ser así by Luis J. Rodríguez. Daniel Galvez, ill. Children's Book Press, 1999. 2.0/K-3
A boy becomes involved in the activities of a local gang until a tragic event involving his cousin forces him to make a choice.
Américas Commended 1999

Jade and Iron: Latin American Tales from Two Cultures edited by Patricia Aldana. Hugh Hazelton, trans. Luis Garay, ill. Groundwood, 1996. 5.7/5-8
Anthology of stories from countries south of the U.S.
Américas Commended 1996

Jalapeño Bagels by Natasha Wing. Robert Casilla, ill. Atheneum, 1996. 2.0/K-3
For International Day at school, Pablo wants to bring something that reflects the cultures of both his parents.
Américas Commended 1996

James Van DerZee: The Picture Takin' Man by James Haskins. Dodd, 1979. 7-4/7-12
Biography of the black photographer acclaimed for his prints of Harlem.
Coretta Scott King Honor, Author 1980   Carter G. Woodson Outstanding Merit 1980

The Japanese American Family Album by Dorothy Hoobler and Thomas Hoobler. Oxford University Press, 1996. 6.0/5-8
Historical account of the Japanese-American experience.
Carter G. Woodson Honor, Secondary 1997

Jazmin's Notebook by Nikki Grimes. Dial, 1998. 5.8/5-8, 5.8/7-12
Jazmin, an Afro-American teenager who lives with her sister in a Harlem apartment in the 1960s, finds strength in writing poetry and keeping a record of her difficult life.
Coretta Scott King Honor, Author 1999

Josefina by Jeanette Winter. Harcourt Brace, 1996. 2.0/P-2
Counting book inspired by Mexican folk artist Josefina Aguilar, who makes painted clay figures.
Américas Commended 1996

Joseph Had a Little Overcoat by Simms Taback. Random, 1977. Viking, 2000. 1.7/K-3
A very old overcoat is recycled numerous times into a variety of garments.
Sydney Taylor Honor, Younger 1999

Joseph Who Loved the Sabbath by Marilyn Hirsch. Devis Grebu, ill. Viking, 1986. Puffin, 1988. oop. na/K-3
Despite his poverty, Joseph celebrated the seventh day with joy.
Sydney Taylor Winner, Younger 1986

Journey of the Nightly Jaguar by Burton Albert. Robert Roth, ill. Atheneum, 1996. oop. na/K-3
Maya legend in which the sun becomes a jaguar at night, stalking through the jungle until it appears again as the sun in the eastern sky.
Américas Commended 1996

The Journey of Tunuri and the Blue Deer: A Huichol Indian Story by James Endredy. María Hernández de la Cruz, ill. and Casimiro de la Cruz López, ill. Bear Cub Books, 2003. 4.0/3-6
Traditional Huichol folktale in which Tunuri learns his place in the natural world after he meets and follows the magical Blue Deer on an enlightening journey.
Américas Commended 2003

Journeys with Elijah by Barbara Diamond Goldin. Jerry Pinkney, ill. Harcourt, 1999. 5.4/3-6
Eight stories about the Old Testament prophet Elijah, set in a variety of time periods and in places all over the world where Jews have lived.
Sydney Taylor Honor, Older 1999

Juan Bobo: Four Folktales from Puerto Rico by Carmen T. Bernier-Grand. Ernesto Ramos Nieves, ill. HarperCollins, 1994. 2.5/K-3
Latino versions of Foolish John folk tales.
Américas Commended 1994

Juan Bobo and the Horse of Seven Colors: A Puerto Rican Legend by Jan Mike. Charles Reasoner, ill. Troll, 1995. 4.0/K-3
After winning seven wishes from a magical horse, foolish Juan Bobo wastes six on his way to try to make the king's daughter laugh.
Américas Commended 1995

Juan Bobo Goes to Work: A Puerto Rican Folktale by Marisa Montes. Joe Cepeda, ill. HarperCollins, 2000. 2.0/K-3
Although he tries to do exactly as his mother tells him, foolish Juan Bobo keeps getting things all wrong.
Pura Belpré Honor, Illustration 2002

The Jumping Tree: A Novel by René Saldaña, Jr. Delacorte Press, 2001.
5.1/5-8, 6.0/5-8
Rey, a Mexican American living with his close-knit family in a Texas town near the Mexican border, describes his transition from boy to young man.
Américas Commended 2001

Junius Over Far by Virginia Hamilton. Harper, 1985. oop. na/ya
After his grandfather leaves his family and returns to a dangerous situation on his home island in the Caribbean, Junius decides to follow him in search of his lost heritage.
Coretta Scott King Honor, Author 1986

Just a Minute: A Trickster Tale and Counting Book by Yuyi Morales.
Chronicle Books, 2003. 2.0/K-3
Señor Calavera arrives at Grandma Beetle's door to take her to the next life, but after helping her count as she makes birthday preparations, he changes his mind.
Américas Winner 2003   Pura Belpré Winner, Illustration 2004
Tomás Rivera Winner 2003

Just Us Women by Jeanette Caines. Pat Cummings, ill. Harper, 1982.
2.0/K-3
A girl and her favorite aunt share the excitement of planning a very special car trip for just the two of them.
Coretta Scott King Honor, Illustrator 1983

Justice and Her Brothers by Virginia Hamilton. Greenwillow, 1978.
Harcourt, 1989. oop. na/4-6
An 11-year-old and her older twin brothers struggle to understand their supersensory powers.
Coretta Scott King Honor, Author 1979

Justin and the Best Biscuits in the World by Mildred Pitts Walter.
Catherine Stock, ill. Lothrop, 1986. 4.0/3-6
Suffering in a family full of females, Justin feels that cleaning and keeping house are women's work until he spends time on his grandfather's ranch.
Coretta Scott King Winner, Author 1987

The Keeping Quilt by Patricia Polacco. Simon & Schuster, 1988, 1998. 2.0/K-3, 4.4/K-3
A homemade quilt ties together the lives of four generations of an immigrant Jewish family, a symbol of their enduring love and faith.
Sydney Taylor Winner, Younger 1988

The Key Is Lost by Ida Vos. Terese Edelstein, trans. HarperCollins, 2000. 5.5/5-8
In 1940 when the Germans occupy Holland and persecute the Jews, Eva and her family assume false names and move from one hiding place to another.
Sydney Taylor Winner, Older 2000

Konnichiwa! I Am a Japanese-American Girl by Tricia Brown. Kazuyoshi Arai, ill. Henry Holt, 1995. oop. na/2-5
Lauren Kamiya tells about her life and family in San Francisco.
Carter G. Woodson Outstanding Merit, Elementary 1996

The Land by Mildred Taylor. Penguin Putnam, 2001. 5.0/5-8
After the Civil War, Paul, son of a white father and black mother, is caught between the two worlds as he pursues his dream of owning land.
Coretta Scott King Winner, Author 2002

Langston Hughes by Milton Meltzer. Stephen Alcorn, ill. Millbrook Press, 1997. 7.2/5-8
Story of a leading poet of the 1920s Harlem Renaissance who devoted his life to writing about the black experience in America.
Carter G. Woodson Winner, Secondary 1998

The Last Princess: The Story of Princess Ka'Iolani of Hawai'i by Fay Stanley. Diane Stanley, ill. Macmillan, 1991, 1994. HarperCollins, 2001. 6.4/3-6
Story of Hawaii's last heir to the throne who was denied her right to rule when the monarchy was abolished.
Carter G. Woodson Winner, Elementary 1992

Laughing Out Loud, I Fly: Poems in English and Spanish by Juan Felipe Herrera. Karen Barbour, ill. HarperCollins, 1998. 6.0/5-8
Poems about childhood, place, and identity.
Pura Belpré Honor, Narrative 2000

Laughing Tomatoes and Other Spring Poems/Jitomates Risueños y otros poemas de primavera by Francisco X. Alarcón. Maya Christina González, ill. Children's Book Press, 1997. 3.0/3-6
Bilingual humorous and serious poems about family, nature, and celebrations by a Mexican-American poet.
Américas Commended 1997   Pura Belpré Honor, Narrative 1998

The Legend of Africania by Dorothy W. Robinson. Herbert Temple, ill. Johnson Publishing, 1974. oop. na/K-3
Allegorical tale of Africa's struggle against the ravishment of its people and country.
Coretta Scott King Winner, Author 1975

The Legend of the Poinsettia by Tomie De Paola. G. P. Putnam's Sons, 1994. 2.0/K-3, 3.6/K-3
A miracle helps Lucinda with a beautiful flower to give the baby Jesus for Christmas.
Américas Commended 1994

Lena Horne by James Haskins. Coward-McCann, 1983. 8.7/ya
Biography of African-American singer and entertainer.
Coretta Scott King Honor, Author 1984

Leon's Story by Leon Walter Tillage. Susan I. Roth, ill. Farrar, Straus & Giroux, 1997. 4.0/3-6, 4.9/3-6
Sharecropper's son recalls hard times faced by his family and other African Americans in the early twentieth century and changes the civil rights movement helped bring about.
Carter G. Woodson Winner, Elementary 1998

Let It Shine! Stories of Black Women Freedom Fighters by Andrea Davis Pinkney. Stephen Alcorn, ill. Harcourt, 2001. 7.2/3-6
Biographical sketches of ten African-American civil rights activists.
Carter G. Woodson Winner, Middle Level 2001   Coretta Scott King Honor, Author 2001

Let the Circle Be Unbroken by Mildred D. Taylor. Dial, 1981. 5.7/7-12, 8.0/7-12
Four black children growing up in Mississippi during the Depression experience racial antagonisms but learn from their parents the pride and self-respect they need to survive.
Coretta Scott King Winner, Author 1982

Let the Lion Eat Straw by Ellease Southerland/Ebele Oseye. Scribner, 1979. G. K. Hall, 1979. na/ya
Story of a troubled African-American family.
Coretta Scott King Honor, Author 1980

Letters from Rifka by Karen Hesse. Henry Holt, 1992. Puffin, 1993. 4.2/3-6
In letters to her cousin, a Jewish girl chronicles her family's flight from Russia in 1919 and her experiences when she is left in Belgium while the others go to America.
Sydney Taylor Winner, Older 1992

A Library for Juana: The World of Sor Juana Inés by Pat Mora. Beatriz Vidal, ill. Knopf, 2002. 2.0/K-3, 3.7/K-3
Biography of the seventeenth-century Mexican poet, learned in many subjects, who became a nun later in life.
Américas Commended 2002   Tomás Rivera Winner 2002

The Life and Death of Crazy Horse by Russell Freedman. Amos Bad Heart Bull, ill. Holiday House, 1996. 7.2/7-12
Oglala leader who resisted the white man's attempts to take over Indian lands.
Carter G. Woodson Honor, Elementary 1997

Life in a Japanese American Internment Camp by Diane Yancey.
Lucent Books, 1998. na/4-6
Japanese immigration into the United States, relocation of Japanese
Americans during World War II, and conditions they faced in the
internment camps.
Carter G. Woodson Honor, Secondary 1999

Lights on the River by Jane Resh Thomas. Michael Dooling, ill.
Hyperion, 1994. oop. na/K-3
Teresa, daughter of Mexican-American migrant workers, has a hard life
but keeps memories of her grandmother and Mexico alive in her heart.
Américas Commended 1994

Like Sisters on the Homefront by Rita Williams-Garcia. Delacorte,
1995. 4.5/7-12, 8.0/7-12
Troubled Gayle is sent down South to live with her uncle and aunt,
where her life begins to change as she experiences the healing power
of the family.
Coretta Scott King Honor, Author 1996

Liliana's Grandmothers by Leyla Torres. Farrar, Straus & Giroux,
1998. 3.3/K-3
Because one of her grandmothers lives down the street and the other in
a far-away country, Liliana experiences two different ways of life when
she visits them.
Américas Commended 1998

Lion and the Ostrich Chicks and Other African Folk Tales by Ashley
Bryan. Atheneum, 1986. 4.0/3-6
Four traditional tales told by the Hausa, Angolan, Masai, and Bushmen
people of Africa.
Coretta Scott King Honor, Author 1987   Coretta Scott King Honor,
Illustrator 1987

The Little Blue House by Sandra Comino. Groundwood, 2003. 4.0/3-6
In a small Argentinean town Cintea finds comfort in a magical white
house that turns blue once a year.
Américas Commended 2003

Little Eight John by Jan Wahl. Wil Clay, ill. Lodestar, 1992. 2.0/K-3
Little Eight John, as mean as mean there was, persists in disobeying his
mother until he finds his mischief backfiring on him.
Coretta Scott King Honor, Illustrator 1993

A Little Love by Virginia Hamilton. Philomel, 1984. oop. na/ya
Though she has been raised lovingly by her grandparents, a black
teenager goes in search of her father.
Coretta Scott King Honor, Author 1985

The Little Painter of Sabana Grande by Patricia Maloney Markun.
Robert Casilla, ill. Bradbury, 1993. 2.0/P-2
Lacking paper, a Panamanian artist paints the outside of his adobe
house.
Américas Commended 1993

A Little Salmon for Witness: A Story from Trinidad by Vashanti
Rahaman. Sandra Speidel, ill. Lodestar, 1997. oop. na/K-3
On Good Friday, a school holiday in Trinidad, Rajiv spends the day
searching for a special birthday present for his grandmother.
Américas Commended 1997

Living in Two Worlds by Maxine B. Rosenberg. George Ancona, ill.
Lothrop, 1986. oop. na/ya
Photo essay about the world of biracial children, who experience the
advantages of two cultures but also face problems and prejudices.
Carter G. Woodson Outstanding Merit 1987

*The Lizard and the Sun/La Largartija y El Sol: A Folktale in English
and Spanish* by Alma Flor Ada. Felipe Dávalos, ill. Rosa Zubizarreta,
trans. Doubleday Dell, 1997. 2.0/K-3
Traditional Mexican folktale in which a lizard finds the sun which
brings light and warmth back to the world.
Américas Commended 1997

Locomotion by Jacqueline Woodson. G. P. Putnam's Sons, 2003. 4.7/5-8
In a series of poems, Lonnie writes about his life, the death of his
parents, separation from his younger sister, living in a foster home, and
finding his poetic voice at school.
Coretta Scott King Honor, Author 2004

Lolo & Red Legs by Kirk Reeve. Rising Moon, 1998. 4.2/3-6
Lolo captures a tarantula and turns that summer into a series of
adventures that take him and his friends beyond their Mexican-
American neighborhood in East Los Angeles.
Américas Commended 1998

A Long Hard Journey: The Story of the Pullman Porter by Patricia C.
McKissack and Fredrick L. McKissack. Walker, 1989. 6.5/5-8
Chronicle of the first black-controlled union of Pullman porters, who
after years of unfair labor practices staged a battle against a corporate
giant.
Coretta Scott King Winner, Author 1990   Carter G. Woodson
Outstanding Merit, Secondary 1990

Lou in the Limelight by Kristin Hunter Lattany. Scribner, 1981. oop.
na/7-9
Lou and the Soul Brothers leave home hoping for quick success in
show business.
Coretta Scott King Honor, Author 1982

Love You, Soldier by Amy Hest. Sonja Lamut, ill. Four Winds, 1991.
Candlewick Press, 2000. Puffin, 1993. 4.0/3-6
Katie, a Jewish girl in New York City during World War II, sees many
changes in her world as she ages from seven to ten waiting for her
father to return from the war.
Sydney Taylor Honor, Older 2000

Madam C. J. Walker: Self-Made Millionaire by Patricia C. McKissack
and Fredrick L. McKissack. Michael Bryant, ill. Enslow, 1992, 2001.
3.6/3-6
Life of a black laundress who founded a cosmetics company and
became the first female self-made millionaire in the United States.
Carter G. Woodson Winner, Elementary 1993

The Magic Bean Tree: A Legend from Argentina by Nancy Van Laan. Beatriz Vidal, ill. Houghton Mifflin, 1998. 3.7/K-3
A Quechuan boy sets out to bring the rains back to his parched homeland and is rewarded by a gift of carob beans that come to be prized across Argentina.
Américas Commended 1998

The Magic Feather: A Jamaican Legend by Lisa Rojany. Philip Kuznicki, ill. Troll, 1995. oop. na/K-3
Solidae must pull a feather from the dreaded Mancrow to bring color and light back to Jamaica.
Américas Commended 1995

The Magic Maguey by Tony Johnson. Elisa Kleven, ill. Harcourt Brace, 1996. oop. na/K-3
Miguel finds a way to save the beloved maguey plant in his Mexican pueblo.
Américas Commended 1996

Magic Windows/Ventanas mágicas by Carmen Lomas Garza. Francisco X. Alarcón, trans. Children's Book Press, 1999. 5.0/3-6
Lomas Garza portrays her family's Mexican-American customs through cut-paper work.
Américas Honorable Mention 1999   Carter G. Woodson Honor, Elementary 2000   Pura Belpré Winner, Illustration 2000

The Magical Adventures of Pretty Pearl by Virginia Hamilton. Harper & Row, 1983. 5.0/7-12
Pretty Pearl, an African god child eager to show off her powers, travels to the New World where, disguised as a human, she lives among a band of free blacks.
Coretta Scott King Honor, Author 1984

Make a Joyful Noise Unto the Lord: The Life of Mahalia Jackson, Queen of the Gospel Singers by Jesse Jackson. Crowell, 1974. G. K. Hall, 1974. oop. na/ya
Biography of the famous black gospel singer who hoped, through her art, to break down barriers between black and white people.
Carter G. Woodson Winner 1975

Malcolm X: By Any Means Necessary: A Biography by Walter Dean Myers. Scholastic, 1993. 6.0/5-8, 8.0/7-12
Biography of a Black Muslim and his impact on the civil rights movement.
Coretta Scott King Honor, Author 1994

Mama and Papa Have a Store by Amelia Lau Carling. Dial, 1998. 4.1/K-3
A girl describes a day in her parents' Chinese store in Guatemala City.
Américas Winner 1998   Pura Belpré Honor, Illustration 2000

Mama Does the Mambo by Katherine Leiner. Edel Rodríguez, ill. Hyperion, 2001. 1.0/P-2
Following the death of her Papa, Sophia fears that her Mama will never find another dancing partner for Carnival.
Américas Commended 2001

Many Thousand Gone—African Americans from Slavery to Freedom by Virginia Hamilton. Leo Dillon, ill. and Diane Dillon, ill. Knopf, 1993. 4.0/3-6, 7.0/5-8
Journeys of slaves to freedom via the underground railroad and the people who helped.
Carter G. Woodson Outstanding Merit, Secondary 1994

The March on Washington by James Haskins. HarperCollins, 1993. 7.6/3-8, 8.9/3-8
People and events of the 1963 March on Washington and consequences of this well-known civil rights demonstration.
Carter G. Woodson Winner, Secondary 1994

Marian Anderson by Charles Patterson. Franklin Watts, 1988. oop.
na/ya
Biography of an opera and concert singer, the first black soloist to
perform with the Metropolitan Opera Company in 1955.
Carter G. Woodson Outstanding Merit, Secondary 1989

La Mariposa by Francisco Jiménez. Simón Silva, ill. Houghton Mifflin,
1998. 2.0/K-3, 4.6/3-6
Because he speaks only Spanish, Francisco has trouble with first grade,
but his fascination with a caterpillar in the classroom helps him begin
to fit in.
Américas Commended 1998

Marisol and Magdalena: The Sound of Our Sisterhood by Veronica
Chambers. Hyperion, 1998. 6.0/5-8
Separated from her best friend in Brooklyn, Marisol spends a year with
her grandmother in Panama where she secretly searches for her father.
Américas Commended 1998

The Market Wedding by Cary Fagan. Regolo Ricci, ill. Tundra Books,
2000. 3.8/3-6
A fishmonger falls in love with a milliner and schemes about a fine
wedding and gifts.
Sydney Taylor Honor, Younger 2000

Martin Luther King, Jr.: Man of Peace by Lillie Patterson. Garrard,
1969. oop. na/ya
Biography of civil rights leader.
Coretta Scott King Winner, Author 1970

Martin Luther King, Jr. and the Freedom Movement by Lillie Patterson.
Facts on File, 1989. 7.0/7-12
Account of the work of Martin Luther King, Jr.
Coretta Scott King Honor, Author 1990

Martin's Big Words: The Life of Dr. Martin Luther King, Jr. by Doreen
Rappaport. Bryan Collier, ill. Hyperion, 2001. 3.4/3-6
Life story of African American civil rights activist.
Coretta Scott King Honor, Illustrator 2002

Marvin & Tige by Frankcina Glass. St. Martin's, 1977. oop. na/ya
Eleven-year-old Tige is taken in by a lonely, disillusioned man and a
friendship develops.
Coretta Scott King Honor, Author 1978

Mary: An Autobiography by Mary E. Mebane. Viking, 1981. na/ya
Autobiography of an African-American woman's life.
Coretta Scott King Honor, Author 1982

Mary McLeod Bethune by Eloise Greenfield. Jerry Pinkney, ill.
Crowell, 1977. na/1-4
Biography of Bethune who made numerous contributions to education
for Afro-Americans.
Coretta Scott King Honor, Author 1978

Master of Mahogany: Tom Day, Free Black Cabinetmaker by Mary E.
Lyons. Charles Scribner's Sons, 1994. 6.4/3-6
Biography of a nineteenth-century craftsman.
Carter G. Woodson Outstanding Merit, Elementary 1995

Matthew Henson: Co-Discoverer of the North Pole by Laura Baskes
Litwin. Enslow, 2001. 7.6/7-12, 8.9/ya
Biography of an African-American explorer.
Carter G. Woodson Honor, Middle Level 2002

Maya Angelou: More Than a Poet by Elaine Slivinski Lisandrelli.
Enslow, 1996. oop. na/ya
Life of a multi-faceted African-American poet, author, and educator.
Carter G. Woodson Honor, Elementary 1997

Mayeros: A Yucatec Maya Family by George Ancona. William Morrow,
1997. oop. na/3-6
Life and customs of Mayan descendants now living in the Yucatan
Peninsula of Mexico.
Américas Honorable Mention 1997

Me in the Middle by Ana María Machado. Caroline Merola, ill. David Unger, trans. Groundwood, 2002. 4.0/3-6
Bel hears her great-grandmother's voice inside her head after she becomes enchanted with a photograph.
Américas Commended 2002

The Meaning of Consuelo by Judith Ortiz Cofer. Farrar, Straus & Giroux, 2003. 6.8/7-12
In 1950s Puerto Rico, Consuelo, the serious daughter, watches her younger sister Mili's tragic disintegration while the family falls apart.
Américas Winner 1994

Mediopollito/Half-Chicken by Alma Flor Ada. Kim Howard, ill. Rosa Zubizarreta, trans. Doubleday, 1995. 3.3/K-3
Mexican folktale that explains why the weather vane has a rooster that spins around.
Américas Commended 1995

Meet Danitra Brown by Nikki Grimes. Floyd Cooper, ill. Lothrop, Lee & Shepard, 1994. 3.4/K-3
An African-American girl sings the praises of her best friend in a series of poems.
Coretta Scott King Honor, Illustrator, 1995

The Mermaid's Twin Sister: More Stories from Trinidad by Lynn Joseph. Donna Perrone, ill. Clarion, 1994. oop. na/3-7
Six short stories set in Trinidad.
Américas Winner 1994

Messengers of Rain and Other Poems from Latin America edited by Claudia M. Lee. Rafael Yockteng, ill. Groundwood, 2002. 4.0/3-6, 6.0/5-8
Anthology of Latin American poetry.
Américas Commended 2002

Mexico and the United States, Their Linked Destinies by E. B. Fincher. Crowell, 1983. oop. na/ya
A study of the historical relationship between the United States and Mexico, with emphasis on Mexico's emerging role as a world leader.
Carter G. Woodson Winner 1984

Mexico's Marvelous Corn/El Maravilloso Maiz de Mexico by Margarita González-Jensen. Rigby, 1997. oop. na/K-3
Examines the growth and uses of corn.
Américas Commended 1997

The Middle Passage: White Ships Black Cargo by Tom Feelings. Dial, 1995. 7.0/7-12
Narrative of the slave trade.
Coretta Scott King Winner, Illustrator 1996

Minty: A Story of Young Harriet Tubman by Alan Schroeder. Jerry Pinkney, ill. Dial, 1996. 3.6/K-3
Young Harriet Tubman, whose childhood name was Minty, dreams of escaping slavery on a plantation in the late 1820s.
Coretta Scott King Winner, Illustrator 1997

Miracle's Boys by Jacqueline Woodson. Putnam, 2000. 4.3/5-8
Lafayette's close relationship with his brother Charlie changes after Charlie is released from a detention home and blames Lafayette for their mother's death.
Coretta Scott King Winner, Author 2001

Mirandy and Brother Wind by Patricia C. McKissack. Jerry Pinkney, ill. Knopf, 1988. 2.0/K-3, 3.6/P-2
To win first prize in the Junior Cakewalk, Mirandy tries to capture the wind for her partner.
Coretta Scott King Winner, Illustrator 1989

Miro in the Kingdom of the Sun by Jane Kurtz. David Frampton, ill. Houghton Mifflin, 1996. oop. na/K-3
An Inca girl succeeds where her brothers and others have failed because her bird friends help her find the special water that will cure the king's son.
Américas Commended 1996

The "Mississippi Burning" Civil Rights Murder Conspiracy Trial: A Headline Court Case by Harvey Fireside. Enslow, 2002. 9.8/7-12
Trial of those accused of murdering three civil rights workers in Mississippi in 1964.
Carter G. Woodson Winner, Secondary 2003

Mississippi Challenge by Mildred Pitts Walter. Bradbury, 1992. 7.0/7-12
The struggle for civil rights for the blacks in Mississippi, from slavery to the signing of the Voting Rights Act in 1965.
Coretta Scott King Honor, Author 1993   Carter G. Woodson Winner, Secondary 1993

Momentos Mágicos: Tales from Latin America Told in English and Spanish by Olga Loya. Carmen Lizardi-Rivera, trans. August House, 1997. 5.0/3-6
Fifteen traditional Latin American tales.
Américas Commended 1998

Money-Hungry by Sharon G. Flake. Hyperion, 2001. 4.0/3-6, 6.0/5-8
All Raspberry can think of is making money so that she and her mother will never have to live on the streets again.
Coretta Scott King Honor, Author 2002

Monster by Walter Dean Myers. Christopher Myers, ill. HarperCollins, 1999. 5.1/7-12
On trial as an accomplice to a murder, Steve records his experiences in prison and in the courtroom as a film script while trying to come to terms with his life.
Coretta Scott King Honor, Author 2000

Morning Star, Black Sun: The Northern Cheyenne Indians and America's Energy Crisis by Brent Ashabranner. Paul Conklin, ill. Dodd Mead, 1982. oop. na/ya
Relations between the Northern Cheyenne of Montana and the U.S. government and the tribe's fight to save its lands from strip-mining coal companies.
Carter G. Woodson Winner 1983

The Moses Basket by Jenny Koralek. Pauline Baynes, ill. Eerdmans, 2003. 4.2/K-3
Biblical account of how Moses was saved and rescued by Pharaoh's daughter.
Sydney Taylor Honor, Younger 2003

Mother Crocodile/Maman Caïman: An Uncle Amadou Tale from Senegal by Birago Diop. Adapted by Rosa Guy. John Steptoe, ill. Delacorte, 1981. oop. na/K-3
Because Mother Crocodile tells stories of the past, the little crocodiles choose to believe she is crazy until they learn otherwise when it is almost too late.
Coretta Scott King Winner, Illustrator 1982

Motown and Didi by Walter Dean Myers. Viking, 1984. 5.1/5-8
Motown and Didi, two loners in Harlem, become allies in a fight against the drug dealer whose dope is destroying Didi's brother.
Coretta Scott King Winner, Author 1985

A Movie in My Pillow/Una pelicula en mi almohada by Jorge Argueta. Elizabeth Gómez, ill. Children's Book Press, 2001. 3.2/3-6
Jorgito lives in San Francisco but remembers his native El Salvador.
Américas Winner 2001

Movin' Up: Pop Gordy Tells His Story by Berry Gordy. Harper & Row, 1979. oop. na/ya
Autobiography of the son of a slave and father of the founder of Motown Records.
Coretta Scott King Honor, Author 1980

Mrs. Moskowitz and the Sabbath Candlesticks by Amy Schwartz. Jewish Publication Society, 1983. na/K-4
Mrs. Moskowitz is unhappy in her new apartment until the discovery of her old Sabbath candlesticks prompts her to turn her new dwelling into a real home.
Sydney Taylor Winner, Younger 1984

Mufaro's Beautiful Daughters: An African Tale by John Steptoe. Lothrop, 1987. 2.0/K-3, 4.3/K-3, 6.0/K-3
Mufaro's two beautiful daughters, one bad-tempered, one kind and sweet, go before the king, who is choosing a wife.
Coretta Scott King Winner, Illustrator 1988

Multiethnic Teens and Cultural Identity by Bárbara C. Cruz. Enslow, 2001. 7.0/7-12
Issues facing teens of multiethnic descent, including discrimination and the search for ethnic identity in an unsympathetic culture.
Carter G. Woodson Winner, Secondary 2002

Murals: Walls That Sing by George Ancona. Marshall Cavendish, 2003. 4.0/3-6
Photo essay about murals, a form of art Ancona regards as authentically para el pueblo (for the people).
Américas Commended 2003

My Daughter, My Son, the Eagle, the Dove: An Aztec Chant by Ana Castillo. Susan Guevara, ill. Dutton, 2000. 2.0/K-3, 4.0/3-6
Poetic celebration of rites of passage.
Américas Commended 2000

My Diary from Here to There/Mi diario de aquí hasta allá by Amada Irma Pérez. Maya Christina González, ill. Children's Book Press, 2002. 4.0/3-6
A girl describes her feelings when her father leaves their home in Mexico to look for work in the U. S.
Américas Commended 2002   Pura Belpré Honor, Narrative 2004

My First Book of Proverbs/Mi Primer Libro de Dichos by Ralfka González and Ana Ruiz. Children's Book Press, 1995. 2.0/K-3, 3.0/3-6 Humorous contemporary illustrations of traditional Mexican-American proverbs in English and Spanish.
Américas Commended 1995

My Grandmother's Stories: A Collection of Jewish Folktales by Adèle Geras. Jael Jordan, ill. Knopf, 1990, 2003. 4.0/3-6 Jewish folktales.
Sydney Taylor Winner, Older 1990

My Land Sings: Stories from the Rio Grande by Rudolfo Anaya. Amy Córdova, ill. Morrow, 1999. 4.9/5-8 Ten original and traditional stories set in New Mexico.
Tomás Rivera Winner 1999

My Mama Needs Me by Mildred Pitts Walter. Pat Cummings, ill. Lothrop, 1983. oop. na/K-3 Jason wants to help but isn't sure that his mother needs him after she brings home a new baby from the hospital.
Coretta Scott King Winner, Illustrator 1984

My Mexico/México mío by Tony Johnston. F. John Sierra, ill. Putnam's, 1996. 2.0/K-3, 2.1/K-3 Poetic and artistic depictions of Mexico.
Américas Commended 1996

My Rows and Piles of Coins by Tololwa M. Mollel. E. B. Lewis, ill. Clarion, 1999. 3.8/K-3 A Tanzanian boy saves coins to buy a bicycle to help his parents carry goods to market but discovers that he does not have enough.
Coretta Scott King Honor, Illustrator 2000

My Two Worlds by Ginger Gordon. Martha Cooper, ill. Clarion, 1993. oop. na/3-6 Contrasts the worlds of a Dominican-American girl who lives in New York City, speaks Spanish as her native language, and frequently returns to her island home.
Américas Commended 1994

My Very Own Room/Mi propio cuartito by Amada Irma Pérez. Maya Christina González, ill. Children's Book Press, 2000. 3.9/3-6
With the help of her family, a Mexican-American girl realizes her dream of having a space of her own.
Américas Honorable Mention 2000   Tomás Rivera Winner 2000

The Mysterious Visitor: Stories of the Prophet Elijah by Nina Jaffe. Elivia Savadier, ill. Scholastic, 1997. oop. na/1-4, na/4-6
Eight stories involving the Biblical prophet Elijah.
Sydney Taylor Winner, Older 1997

Nathaniel Talking by Eloise Greenfield. Jan Spivey Gilchrist, ill. Black Butterfly, 1988. 4.0/3-6
Eighteen first-person poems from Nathaniel's point of view.
Coretta Scott King Honor, Author 1990   Coretta Scott King Winner, Illustrator 1990

Native American Doctor: The Story of Susan LaFlesche Picotte by Jeri Ferris. Carolrhoda Books, 1991. 6.6/5-8
Biography of the first Native-American woman to graduate from medical school.
Carter G. Woodson Winner, Secondary 1992

Native American Testimony: An Anthology of Indian and White Relations: First Encounter to Dispossession edited by Peter Nabokov. Crowell, 1978. Harper & Row, 1984. Viking, 1991. na/ya
Documents in which Native Americans describe their responses to explorers, traders, missionaries, settlers, government diplomats, and soldiers seeking dominion over them.
Carter G. Woodson Winner 1979

Neeny Coming, Neeny Going by Karen English. Synthia Saint James, ill. BridgeWater Books, 1996. 2.0/K-3
Essie eagerly awaits the visit of her cousin but is disheartened after her arrival because Neeny is no longer interested in life on the island from which she moved.
Coretta Scott King Honor, Illustrator 1997

Never to Forget: The Jews of the Holocaust by Milton Meltzer. Harper & Row, 1976. 8.2/6-12
An account of the Jewish Holocaust.
Sydney Taylor Winner 1976

New Kids on the Block: Oral Histories of Immigrant Teens by Janet Bode. Franklin Watts, 1989. oop. na/ya
Teenage immigrants recount their emotional experiences fleeing their homelands and adjusting to new lives in the United States.
Carter G. Woodson Outstanding Merit, Secondary 1990

The Night Journey by Kathryn Lasky. Trina Schart Hyman, ill. F. Warne, 1981. Puffin, 1986. 5.3/5-8
Rache ignores her parents' wishes and persuades her great-grandmother to tell the story of her escape from czarist Russia.
Sydney Taylor Winner, Older 1981

Night on Neighborhood Street by Eloise Greenfield. Jan Spivey Gilchrist, ill. Dial, 1991. 3.2/3-6
Poems exploring the sounds, sights, and emotions enlivening one evening in a black neighborhood.
Coretta Scott King Honor, Author 1992   Coretta Scott King Honor, Illustrator 1992

Nina Bonita by Ana María Machado. Rosana Faría, ill. Elena Iribarren, trans. Kane/Miller, 1996. 2.0/K-3, 3.7/P-2
Enchanted by Nina Bonita's black skin, a white rabbit determines to find a way to have children as beautiful and black as she.
Américas Commended 1996

Nine Spoons by Marci Stillerman. Pesach Gerber, ill. HaChai Publishers, 1998. 2.0/K-3
Brave souls in a Nazi camp are determined to gather nine spoons to make a menorah for Chanukah.
Sydney Taylor Winner, Younger 1998

Noah and the Great Flood by Mordicai Gerstein. Simon & Schuster, 1999. 4.0/3-6
Old Testament story of how Noah and his family were saved, along with two of every living creature, when God destroyed the wicked of the world with a flood.
Sydney Taylor Honor, Younger 1999

Noah's Ark by Jerry Pinkney. SeaStar Books, 2002. 3.3/K-3
Biblical story of the great flood and how Noah and his family faithfully responded to God's call to save life on earth.
Sydney Taylor Honor, Younger 2002

Not a Copper Penny in Me House: Poems from the Caribbean by Monica Gunning. Frané Lessac, ill. Wordsong/Boyds Mills Press, 1993. 3.9/K-3, 3.9/1-5
Poems describing the activities of children living on a Caribbean Island.
Américas Commended 1994

Novio Boy: A Play by Gary Soto. Harcourt, 1997. 7.0/7-12
Rudy prepares for and goes out on a date with an attractive girl who is older than he.
Américas Commended 1997

Now Is Your Time! The African American Struggle for Freedom by Walter Dean Myers. HarperCollins, 1991. 8.3/5-8
History of the African-American struggle for freedom and equality, beginning in 1619, through the American Revolution, the Civil War, to contemporary times.
Coretta Scott King Winner, Author 1992   Carter G. Woodson Outstanding Merit, Secondary 1992

The Number on My Grandfather's Arm by David Adler. Rose Eichenbaum, ill. UAHC Press, 1987. 2.0/K-3
A girl questions a number printed on her grandfather's arm, and he explains how he received it in a Nazi concentration camp during World War II.
Sydney Taylor Winner, Younger 1987.

Number the Stars by Lois Lowry. Houghton Mifflin, 1989. 4.0/3-6, 4.5/3-6, 6.0/5-8
In 1943 during the German occupation of Denmark, Annemarie learns to be courageous when she helps shelter her Jewish friend from the Nazis.
Sydney Taylor Winner, Older 1989

Old Letivia and the Mountain of Sorrows by Nicholasa Mohr. Rudy Gutiérrez, ill. Viking, 1996. 5.1/K-3
To end the devastation of a Puerto Rican town, Old Letivia and her friends use her magic to conquer evil forces.
Américas Commended 1996

The Old Man and His Door by Gary Soto. Joe Cepeda, ill. Putnam's, 1996. 2.0/K-3
Misunderstanding his wife's instructions, an old man sets out for a party with a door on his back.
Américas Commended 1996

One Candle by Eve Bunting. K. Wendy Popp, ill. HarperCollins, 2002. 2.0/K-3, 2.9/K-3
Every year a family celebrates Hanukkah by retelling the story of how Grandma and her sister marked the day while in a German concentration camp.
Sydney Taylor Honor, Older 2002

Only Passing Through: The Story of Sojourner Truth by Anne Rockwell. Gregory Christie, ill. Random House, 2000. 4.0/3-6, 5.2/3-6
Biography of an African-American former slave who campaigned against slavery.
Coretta Scott King Honor, Illustrator 2001

The Origin of Life on Earth: An African Creation Myth retold by David A. Anderson. Kathleen Atkins Wilson, ill. Sights Productions, 1991. na/K-3
Yoruba creation myth in which Obatala descends from the sky to create the world.
Coretta Scott King Winner, Illustrator 1993

The Other Side: Shorter Poems by Angela Johnson. Orchard, 1998.
6.0/5-8
Poems by an African-American woman who grew up in Shorter,
Alabama.
Coretta Scott King Honor, Author 1999

Our Eddie by Sulamith Ish-Kishor. Pantheon, 1969. Knopf, 1992. oop.
8.9/ya
Two young people relate the difficulties of a family in which their
idealistic, religious, and loving father does not understand the needs of
his family.
Sydney Taylor Winner 1969

Our Golda: The Story of Golda Meir by David Adler. Donna Ruff, ill.
Viking, 1984. Puffin, 1986. oop. na/3-6
Biography of an Israeli prime minister and world leader who spent her
childhood and youth in Russia and the U.S.
Carter G. Woodson Outstanding Merit 1985

Outward Dreams: Black Inventors and Their Inventions by James
Haskins. Walker, 1991. 6.0/5-8, 8.0/7-12
Black inventors including Benjamin Bradley, Madam Walker, and
George Washington Carver and their contributions.
Carter G. Woodson Outstanding Merit, Secondary 1992

Over Here It's Different: Carolina's Story by Mildred Leinweber
Dawson. George Ancona, ill. Macmillan, 1993. oop. na/3-6
Experiences of a girl who immigrates from the Dominican Republic,
descriptions of the two worlds she lives in, and her efforts to preserve
her heritage.
Américas Commended 1994

Pablo Remembers: The Fiesta of the Day of the Dead by George
Ancona. Lothrop, Lee & Shepard, 1993. 2.0/K-3, 4.8/K-3, 4.8/3-6
During the three-day celebration of the Days of the Dead, a Mexican
boy and his family make preparations to honor the spirits of the dead.
Pura Belpré Honor, Illustration 1996

Pablo's Tree by Pat Mora. Cecily Lang, ill. Simon & Schuster, 1994.
2.1/P-2
Each year on his birthday, a Mexican-American boy looks forward to
seeing how his grandfather has decorated the tree he planted on the day
the boy was adopted.
Américas Commended 1994

The Palm of My Heart: Poetry by African American Children edited by
Davida Adedjouma. Gregory Christie, ill. Lee & Low, 1996. 2.0/K-3
Poems by Afro-American children celebrating what it means to be
black.
Coretta Scott King Honor, Illustrator 1997

Parrot in the Oven by Victor Martínez. HarperCollins, 1996. 6.1/7-12,
8.0/7-12
Manny relates his coming-of-age experiences as a member of a poor
Mexican-American family in which the alcoholic father adds to
everyone's struggle.
Américas Winner 1996   Pura Belpré Winner, Narrative 1998

Pascual's Magic Pictures by Amy Glaser Gage. Karen Dugan, ill.
Carolrhoda, 1996. oop. na/K-3
Having saved money to buy a camera, Pascual goes into the
Guatemalan jungle to take pictures of monkeys, but the results are not
what he expected.
Américas Commended 1996

The Patchwork Quilt by Valerie Flournoy. Jerry Pinkney, ill. Dial,
1985. 3.7/P-2
Using scraps cut from the family's old clothing, Tanya helps her
grandmother and mother make a beautiful quilt that tells the story of
her family's life.
Coretta Scott King Winner, Illustrator 1986

Paul Robeson, Hero Before His Time by Rebecca Larsen. Franklin
Watts, 1989. oop. na/6-9
Life and career of the singer, actor, and political activist.
Carter G. Woodson Winner, Secondary 1990

Pearl's Passover: A Family Celebration Through Stories, Recipes, Crafts, and Songs by Jane Breskin Zalben. Simon & Schuster, 2002. 2.0/K-3
An extended family prepares for a Passover celebration and explains customs and traditions related to this holiday.
Sydney Taylor Honor, Younger 2002

The Peddler's Gift by Maxine Rose Schur. Kimberly Bulcken Root, ill. Dial, 1999. oop. na/K-3
A boy in turn-of-the-century rural Russia learns that appearances are often deceiving after he steals and then tries to return a dreidel to the traveling peddler Shnook.
Sydney Taylor Winner, Younger 1999

Pedrito's Day by Luis Garay. Orchard, 1997. oop. na/K-3
When Pedrito replaces, from his own earnings, money he has lost, his mother decides that some of his father's earnings will be used to buy him a bicycle.
Américas Commended 1997

Pedro and Me: Friendship, Loss, and What I Learned by Judd Winick. Henry Holt, 2000. 6.3/9-12
In graphic art format, a description of a friendship between two roommates on the MTV show "Real World," one of whom died of AIDS.
Américas Commended 2000

Pedro Fools the Gringo, and Other Tales of a Latin American Trickster by María Cristina Brusca and Toña Wilson. María Cristina Brusca, ill. Henry Holt, 1995. oop. na/3-6
Twelve Latin American trickster tales.
Américas Commended 1995

The People Could Fly: American Black Folktales by Virginia Hamilton. Leo Dillon, ill and Diane Dillon, ill. Knopf, 1985. 2.0/K-3, 4.3/3-6
Afro-American folktales of animals, fantasy, supernatural, and the desire for freedom, born of the sorrow of slaves, but passed on in hope.
Coretta Scott King Winner, Author 1986   Coretta Scott King Honor, Illustrator 1986

People of Corn: A Mayan Story by Mary-Joan Gerson. Carla Golembe, ill. Little, Brown, 1995. oop. na/K-3
After unsuccessful attempts to create grateful creatures, the Mayan gods use sacred corn to fashion a people who will thank and praise their creators.
Américas Commended 1995

Petty Crimes by Gary Soto. Harcourt, 1998. 4.0/3-6
Short stories about Mexican-American youth growing up in California's Central Valley.
Américas Commended 1998

A Picture of Grandmother by Esther Hautzig. Beth Peck, ill. Farrar, Straus & Giroux, 2002. 4.3/3-6
A letter inviting Sara's mother and grandmother to come from Poland to America and a mysterious photograph help Sara discover a family secret.
Sydney Taylor Honor, Older 2002

Platero y Yo/Platero and I by Juan Ramón Jiménez. Selected and translated by Myra Cohn Livingston and Joseph F. Domínguez. Antonio Frasconi, ill. Clarion, 1994. 6.4/3-6
Life in the town of Moguer, in Andalusia, Spain, as seen through the eyes of a wandering poet and his faithful donkey.
Américas Commended 1994

Portia: The Life of Portia Washington Pittman, the Daughter of Booker T. Washington by Ruth Ann Stewart. Doubleday, 1977. oop. na/ya
Biography of Portia Washington Pittman.
Coretta Scott King Honor, Author 1978

The Pot That Juan Built by Nancy Andrew-Goebel. David Díaz, ill. Lee & Low, 2002. 6.2/K-5
Cumulative rhyme summarizes the life and work of renowned Mexican potter, Juan Quezada, and describes the process he uses.
Américas Commended 2002   Pura Belpré Honor, Illustration 2004

Pride Against Prejudice: The Biography of Larry Doby by Joseph Moore. Praeger, 1988. Greenwood, 1988. na/ya
Biography of the first black baseball player in the American League.
Carter G. Woodson Outstanding Merit, Secondary 1989

Prietita and the Ghost Woman/Prietita y la Llorona by Gloria Anzaldúa. Maya Christina González, ill. Children's Book Press, 1995. 3.0/3-6
Prietita, a Mexican-American girl, becomes lost in her search for an herb to cure her mother and is aided by la Llorona, the legendary ghost woman.
Américas Commended 1996

Prince Estabrook: Slave and Soldier by Alice Hinkle. Kirkwood, 2001. oop. na/ya
Biography of an African-American patriot and soldier in the American Revolution.
Carter G. Woodson Winner, Middle Level 2002

Princess Ka'iulani: Hope of a Nation, Heart of a People by Sharon Linnea. Eerdmans, 1999. 6.0/5-8
Biography of Hawaii's last princess.
Carter G. Woodson Winner, Secondary 2000

Princess of the Press: The Story of Ida B. Wells-Barnett by Angela Shelf Medearis. Lodestar, 1997. oop. na/3-5
Biography of the journalist, newspaper owner, and suffragette who campaigned for civil rights and founded the National Association for the Advancement of Colored People.
Carter G. Woodson Honor, Elementary 1998

Pueblo Storyteller by Diane Hoyt-Goldsmith. Lawrence Migdale, ill. Holiday House, 1991. 5.2/3-6
A Cochiti Indian girl living with her grandparents in the Cochiti Pueblo in New Mexico describes her home, family, day-to-day life, and customs.
Carter G. Woodson Outstanding Merit, Elementary 1992

Rabbit Wishes by Linda Shute. Lothrop, Lee & Shepard, 1995. oop.
na/K-3
An Afro-Cuban folk tale that explains why rabbits have long ears.
Américas Commended 1995

Racial Prejudice by Elaine Pasco. Franklin Watts, 1985. oop. na/ya
Discusses the causes and history of prejudice against minority groups
in the U. S., reviewing the damaging effects of prejudice and
suggesting ways to eliminate it.
Carter G. Woodson Outstanding Merit 1986

Radio Man/Don Radio by Arthur Dorros. Sandra Marulanda Dorros,
trans. HarperCollins, 1997. 3.0/3-6
As he travels with his family of migrant farm workers, Diego relies on
his radio to provide companionship and to help connect him to all the
different places in which he lives.
Américas Honorable Mention 1993

Rainbow Jordan by Alice Childress. Coward-McCann, 1981. 4.3/7-12
Her mother, her foster guardian, and Rainbow comment on the state of
things as she prepares to return to a foster home for yet another stay.
Coretta Scott King Honor, Author 1982

Ramadan by Suhaib Hamid Ghazi. Omar Rayyan, ill. Holiday House,
1996. 2.0/K-3
Describes the celebration of the month of Ramadan by an Islamic
family and the meaning and importance of this Islamic religious
holiday.
Carter G. Woodson Winner, Elementary 1997

Ransom for a River Dolphin by Sarita Kendall. Lerner, 1993. oop.
na/ya
Finding a hurt dolphin near her Colombian village and suspecting her
stepfather of wounding it, Carmenza nurses it to health and tries to
appease its spirit.
Américas Commended 1994

Rap A Tap Tap: Here's Bojangels—Think of That! by Leo Dillon and Diane Dillon. Scholastic, 2002. 1.9/P-2, 1.9/K-3
Describes the dancing of Bill "Bojangles" Robinson, a famous tap dancer.
Coretta Scott King Honor, Illustrator 2003

Rata, Pata, Scata, Fata: A Caribbean Story by Phillis Gershator. Holly Meade, ill. Little, Brown, 1994. Joy Street, 1993. oop. na/K-3
Preferring to dream away the days on his Caribbean island, little Junjun tries saying magic words to get the chores done.
Américas Commended 1994

Ray Charles by Sharon Bell Mathis. George Ford, ill. Crowell, 1973. 1.0/P-2
Biography of the black musician who became famous despite his blindness.
Coretta Scott King Winner, Author and Illustrator 1974

Rebels Against Slavery: American Slave Revolts by Patricia C. McKissack and Fredrick L. McKissack. Scholastic, 1996. 6.0/5-8
Historic African-Americans like Nat Turner and others who defied slavery.
Coretta Scott King Honor, Author 1997

The Red Comb by Fernando Pico. María Antonia Ordonez, ill. BridgeWater Books, 1994. oop. na/3-6
In mid-nineteenth-century Puerto Rico, an old woman and a girl conspire to prevent the capture of a runaway African slave.
Américas Commended 1994

The Red Rose Box by Brenda Woods. Putnam, 2002. 4.9/3-6
In 1953 Leah dreams of leaving the poverty and segregation of her Louisiana home so when her aunt sends tickets to Los Angeles for her birthday, she gets a taste of freedom.
Coretta Scott King Honor 2003

Red-Tail Angels: The Story of the Tuskegee Airmen of World War II by Patricia C. McKissack and Fredrick L. McKissack. Walker and Company, 1995. 8.0/7-12
History of African-American pilots with a focus on World War II.
Carter G. Woodson Outstanding Merit, Secondary 1996

Remembering Manzanar: Life in a Japanese Relocation Camp by Michael L. Cooper. Clarion, 2002. 7.4/3-6
Japanese-American accounts of World War II internment camps.
Carter G. Woodson Winner, Middle Level 2003

The Return by Sonia Levitin. Atheneum, 1987. 7.0/7-12
Desta and members of her Falasha family, Jews suffering from discrimination in Ethiopia, flee the country and attempt the dangerous journey to Israel.
Sydney Taylor Winner, Older 1987

The Riches of Oseola McCarty by Evelyn Coleman. Daniel Minter, ill. A. Whitman, 1998. 5.5/2-5, 5.5/4-6
Biography of McCarty, a hard-working washer woman who donated a portion of her life savings to endow a scholarship fund for needy students.
Carter G. Woodson Honor, Elementary 1999

Rio Grande Stories compiled by Carolyn Meyer. Harcourt, 1994. 5.0/3-6
While preparing a book about the people and traditions of the diverse cultures of Albuquerque, seventh-graders discover interesting things about their city and families.
Américas Commended 1994

The Rise and Fall of Jim Crow: The African-American Struggle Against Discrimination, 1865-1954 by Richard Wormser. Franklin Watts, 1999. St. Martin's Press, 2003. 4.0/3-6, 8.6/7-12
Laws and practices that supported discrimination against African Americans, from Reconstruction to the Supreme Court decision that found segregation to be illegal.
Carter G. Woodson Honor, Secondary 2000

Rivka's First Thanksgiving by Elsa Okon Rael. Maryann Kovalski, ill. Simon & Schuster, 2001. 3.9/P-2
Having heard about Thanksgiving in school, Rivka tries to convince her immigrant family and rabbi that it is a holiday for all, Jews and non-Jews alike.
Sydney Taylor Winner, Younger 2001

The Road to Memphis by Mildred D. Taylor. Dial, 1990. Puffin, 1992. 4.5/7-12, 8.0/7-12
Sadistically teased by two white boys in 1940's rural Mississippi, a black youth injures one of the boys and enlists Cassie's help to flee the state.
Coretta Scott King Winner, Author 1991

Roadrunner's Dance by Rudolfo Anaya. David Díaz, ill. Hyperion, 2000. 2.0/K-3
Rattlesnake takes over the road and will not let animals or people in the village use it, so Desert Woman and the other animals create a creature to overcome Rattlesnake.
Américas Commended 2000

Rosa Parks by Eloise Greenfield. Eric Marlow, ill. Crowell, 1973. 4.0/3-6
Biography of the black woman known as the Mother of the Civil Rights Movement because of her part in the Montgomery bus boycott.
Carter G. Woodson Winner 1974

Running the Road to ABC by Denizé Lauture. Reynold Ruffins, ill. Simon & Schuster, 1996. 2.0/K-3, 4.2/K-3
Long before the sun rises, Haitian children run to school where they learn the letters, sounds, and words of their beautiful books.
Américas Commended 1996   Coretta Scott King Honor, Illustrator 1997

A Russian Farewell by Leonard Everett Fisher. Four Winds Press, 1980. oop. na/4-6
Depicts the anti-Semitic terror that drives Benjamin Shapiro, his wife, and children out of Czarist Russia to the U. S. at the beginning of the twentieth century.
Sydney Taylor Winner 1980

Sacagawea by Lise Erdrich. Julie Buffalohead, ill. Carolrhoda Books, 2003. 4.0/3-6
Biography of the Shoshone girl who accompanied Lewis and Clark.
Carter G. Woodson Winner, Elementary 2004

The Sad Night: The Story of an Aztec Victory and a Spanish Loss by Sally Schofer Mathews. Clarion, 1994. 3.0/K-3, 4.0/3-6
How the Aztecs established an empire in Mexico and what happened when they and Montezuma encountered Cortés and the Spaniards in the sixteenth century.
Américas Commended 1994

Salsa Stories by Lulu Delacre. Scholastic, 2000. 5.0/3-6
Stories within the story of a family celebration where guests relate recipes and their memories of growing up in various Latin American countries.
Américas Commended 2000

Sammy Spider's First Trip to Israel: A Book about the Five Senses by Sylvia Rouss. Katherine Janus Kahn, ill. Kar-Ben Publications, 2002. na/K-2, na/1-3
Sammy Spider joins the Shapiro family on a vacation and uses his five senses to experience Israel.
Sydney Taylor Honor, Younger 2002

Saturday Market by Patricia Grossman. Enrique O. Sánchez, ill. Lothrop, Lee & Shepard, 1994. 4.2/P-2
Ana and Estela sell their handmade goods at a Saturday market in Mexico.
Américas Commended 1994

Saturday Sancocho by Leyla Torres. Farrar, Straus & Giroux, 1995. 2.0/K-3
María Lili and her grandmother barter a dozen eggs at the market square to get the ingredients to cook their traditional Saturday chicken sancocho.
Américas Commended 1995

The Secret of Two Brothers by Irene Beltrán Hernández. Piñata Books, 1995. 5.0/6-9, 5.0/7-10
Beaver Torres returns after three years in a detention center ready to help his younger brother and make a good life for them.
Américas Commended 1995

The Secret Stars by Joseph Slate. Felipe Dávalos, ill. Marshall Cavendish, 1998. 2.7/P-2, 2.7/1-3
On a rainy, icy Night of the Three Kings, Sila and Pepe worry that the kings will not be able to use the stars to navigate, but their grandmother takes them on a magical journey.
Américas Commended 1998   Pura Belpré Honor, Illustration 2000

Señor Cat's Romance and Other Favorite Stories from Latin America by Lucia M. González. Lulu Delacre, ill. Scholastic, 1997. 2.9/P-3, 2.9/1-3
Latin-American folklore.
Américas Commended 1997

Sequoyah's Gift: A Portrait of the Cherokee Leader by Janet Klausner. HarperCollins, 1993. 6.6/3-6
Biography of the Cherokee Indian who created a method for his people to write and read their language.
Carter G. Woodson Outstanding Merit, Secondary 1994

Seventeen Black Artists by Elton C. Fax. Dodd, Mead, 1971. oop. na/ya
Biographies of African-American artists.
Coretta Scott King Winner, Author 1972

The Shadow Children by Steven Schnur. Herbert Tauss, ill. Morrow, 1994. 4.9/3-6
During a summer on his grandfather's farm in the French countryside, Etienne discovers a secret from World War II and encounters the ghosts of Jewish children.
Sydney Taylor Winner, Older 1994

Shalom, Haver/Goodbye, Friend by Barbara Sofer. Shulamith Basok, trans. Kar-Ben Copies, 1996. oop. na/3-5
Photo essay in memory of Yitzhak Rabin, the Israeli prime minister assassinated in 1995.
Sydney Taylor Winner, Younger 1996

Shirley Chisholm, Teacher and Congresswoman by Catherine Scheader. Enslow, 1990. oop. na/7-10
Biography of the first black woman to run for president of the U. S.
Carter G. Woodson Winner, Elementary 1991

Sigmund Freud: Pioneer of the Mind by Catherine Reef. Clarion, 2001. 8.5/5-8
Biography of the father of psychoanalysis who changes the world's view of the human mind.
Sydney Taylor Winner, Older 2001

The Singing Man: Adapted from a West African Folktale by Angela Shelf Medearis. Terea Shaffer, ill. Holiday House, 1994. 2.0/P-2
A son is forced to leave his West African village after he chooses music over the practical occupations of his brothers, but he returns to show the wisdom of his choice.
Coretta Scott King Honor, Illustrator 1995

A Single Shard by Linda Sue Park. Clarion Books, 2001. 4.0/3-6, 6.0/5-8, 6.6/5-8
Tree-ear, an orphan in medieval Korea, lives under a bridge in a potters' village and longs to learn how to make delicate celadon ceramics.
Asian Pacific American Honor, Text 2004

Skates of Uncle Richard by Carol Fenner. Ati Forberg, ill. Random, 1978. 3.0/3-6
With her uncle's encouragement a nine-year-old takes a step toward realizing her dream of becoming a figure skater.
Coretta Scott King Honor, Author 1979

Slam! by Walter Dean Myers. Scholastic, 1996. 4.5/7-12
"Slam" Harris is counting on his basketball talents to get him out of the inner city and give him a chance to succeed in life, but his coach sees things differently.
Coretta Scott King Winner, Author 1997

Slavery Time When I Was Chillun edited by Belinda Hurmence. Putnam, 1997. 5.0/5-8
Oral interviews of former slaves; part of a 1936 Slave Narratives project of the Library of Congress and Works Progress Administration.
Carter G. Woodson Honor, Secondary 1998

Smoke and Ashes: The Story of the Holocaust by Barbara Rogasky. Holiday House, 2002. 7.9/5-8
An account of the Jewish Holocaust of World War II.
Sydney Taylor Honor, Older 2002

Snapshots from the Wedding by Gary Soto. Stephanie Garcia, ill. Putnam, 1997. 4.4/K-3
Maya describes a Mexican-American wedding through snapshots of the events, beginning with the procession and ending with her sleeping after the dance.
Pura Belpré Winner, Illustration 1998

So Loud a Silence by Lyll Becerra de Jenkins. Lodestar, 1996. oop. na/6-10
Juan Guillermo feels aloof from his family until he spends time with his grandmother, a landowner in Colombia, and is caught in the fighting between guerrillas and the army.
Américas Winner, 1996

Sojourner Truth: Ain't I a Woman? by Patricia C. McKissack and Fredrick L. McKissack. Scholastic, 1992. 7.0/3-6
Biography of a former slave who became an abolitionist and advocate of women's rights.
Coretta Scott King Honor, Author 1993

Sojourner Truth: From Slave to Activist for Freedom by Mary G. Butler. PowerPlus Books, 2003. 7.8/5-8
Biography of activist Sojourner Truth.
Carter G. Woodson Honor, Middle Level 2004

Something from Nothing: Adapted from a Jewish Folktale by Phoebe Gilman. Scholastic, 1992. 3.3/K-3
Traditional Jewish folktale in which Joseph's baby blanket is transformed into ever smaller items as he grows until there is nothing left, but then Joseph has an idea.
Sydney Taylor Winner, Younger 1992

Something on My Mind by Nikki Grimes. Tom Feelings, ill. Dial, 1978. oop. na/1-6
Poems expressing the hopes, fears, joys, and sorrows of growing up.
Coretta Scott King Winner, Illustrator 1979

Somewhere in the Darkness by Walter Dean Myers. Scholastic, 1992. 4.4/7-12
A boy accompanies his father, escaped from prison, on a trip that becomes an often painful time of discovery for both.
Coretta Scott King Honor, Author 1993

The Song of El Coquí and Other Tales of Puerto Rico. La canción del coquí y otros cuentos de Puerto Rico by Nicholasa Mohr and Antonio Martorell. Viking, 1995. oop. na/K-3
Three folktales reflecting the diverse heritages within the Puerto Rican culture.
Américas Commended 1995

Songs from the Loom: A Navajo Girl Learns to Weave by Monty Roessel. Lerner, 1995. 4.0/3-6, 5.2/3-6
Ten-year-old Jaclyn Roessel learns traditional weaving from her grandmother.
Carter G. Woodson Winner, Elementary 1996

Sorrow's Kitchen: The Life and Folklore of Zora Neale Hurston by Mary E. Lyons. Scribner's, 1990, 1993. 6.9/7-12
Life and work of the prolific black author who wrote stories, plays, essays, and articles, recorded black folklore, and was involved in the Harlem Renaissance.
Carter G. Woodson Winner, Secondary 1991

Soul Looks Back in Wonder by Phyllis Fogelman. Tom Feelings, ill. Dial, 1993. 2.0/K-3, 4.4/3-6
Artwork and poems about Maya Angelou, Langston Hughes, Askia Toure, and others portray the creativity, strength, and beauty of their African-American heritage.
Coretta Scott King Winner, Illustrator 1994

The Sound That Jazz Makes by Carole Boston Weatherford. Eric Velasquez, ill. Walker & Company, 2000. 2.0/K-3, 4.7/3-6
Illustrated history of the origins and influences of jazz, from Africa to contemporary America.
Carter G. Woodson Winner, Elementary 2001

Speed of Light by Sybil Rosen. Atheneum, 1999. 3.9/5-8, 6.0/5-8
A Jewish girl living in the South during the 1950s struggles with anti-Semitism and racism that pervades her community.
Sydney Taylor Winner, Older 1999

The Spirit of Tío Fernando: A Day of the Dead Story. El espíritu de tío Fernando: Una historia del Día de los Muertos by Janice Levy. Morella Fuenmayor, ill. Teresa Mlawer, trans. A. Whitman, 1995. 3.2/K-3
As he prepares to celebrate the Day of the Dead, a boy remembers his favorite uncle.
Américas Commended 1995

Spirits of the High Mesa by Floyd Martínez. Arte Público, 1997. 8.0/7-12
Flavio and his family and friends are beset by changes in their isolated New Mexican village after electricity and a sawmill bring in strangers.
Américas Commended 1997   Pura Belpré Honor, Narrative 1998

Star of Fear, Star of Hope by Jo Hoestlandt. Johanna Kang, ill. Mark Polizzotti, trans. Walker, 1995. 3.3/3-6
Helen is confused by the disappearance of her Jewish friend during the German occupation of Paris.
Sydney Taylor Winner, Younger 1995

Starting Home: The Story of Horace Pippin, Painter by Mary E. Lyons. Charles Scribner's Sons, 1993. oop. na/4-7
Life and work of the African-American folk artist.
Carter G. Woodson Winner, Elementary 1994

A Step from Heaven by An Na. Front Street, 2001. 4.2/7-12, 8.0/7-12
A Korean girl and her family find it difficult to adjust to life in the U. S.
Asian Pacific American Winner, Text 2004

Stones in Water by Donna Jo Napoli. Dutton, 1997. 4.2/5-8
After being taken by German soldiers, Roberto is forced to work in Germany, escapes into the Ukrainian, and makes his way back home to Venice.
Sydney Taylor Winner, Older 1998

Storm in the Night by Mary Stolz. Pat Cummings, ill. Harper, 1988. 3.2/K-3
While sitting through a thunderstorm that has put the lights out, Thomas hears a story from Grandfather's boyhood when he also was afraid of thunderstorms.
Coretta Scott King Honor, Illustrator 1989

The Story of Doña Chila/El cuento de Doña Chila by Mary Capellinni. Gershom Griffith, ill. Rigby, 1997. oop. na/K-3
Story of a medicine woman and the villagers of Honduras.
Américas Commended 1997

The Story of Stevie Wonder by James Haskins. Lothrop, 1976. oop.
na/ya
Biography of the blind composer, pianist, and singer who was a child
prodigy and winner of nine Grammy awards.
Coretta Scott King Winner, Author 1977

Story Painter: The Life of Jacob Lawrence by John Duggleby. Jacob
Lawrence, ill. Chronicle Book, 1998. 6.0/5-8
Biography of the African-American artist who grew up during the
Harlem Renaissance and became a renowned painter of his people.
Carter G. Woodson Winner, Elementary 1999

The Stowaway: A Tale of California Pirates by Kristiana Gregory.
Scholastic, 1995. 5.4/5-8
In 1818 Spanish-owned Monterey, California, Carlito sees his life
threatened when the privateer Hippolyte de Bouchard attacks with
pirate ships.
Américas Commended 1995

Strong Right Arm: The Story of Mamie "Peanut" Johnson by Michelle
Y. Green. Dial Books for Young Readers, 2002. 4.7/5-8
Biography of an African-American woman baseball player who played
in the Negro Leagues.
Carter G. Woodson Honor, Middle Level 2003

Sukey and the Mermaid by Robert D. San Souci. Brian Pinkney, ill.
Four Winds, 1992. 4.8/P-2
Unhappy with her life at home, Sukey receives kindness and wealth
from Mama Jo the mermaid.
Coretta Scott King Honor, Illustrator 1993

Summer on Wheels by Gary Soto. Scholastic, 1995. 4.0/5-8, 6.4/5-8
Hector and his friend Mondo take a six-day bike trip from their East
Los Angeles neighborhood to the Santa Monica beach.
Américas Commended 1995

A Sunburned Prayer by Marc Talbert. Simon & Schuster, 1995. 5.4/5-8
As he makes a pilgrimage to the Santuario de Chimayó to save his grandmother from cancer, Eloy is joined by a friendly dog that helps him keep going.
Américas Commended 1995

Sweet Fifteen by Diane Gonzáles Bertrand. Piñata Books, 1995. 8.0/7-12
When seamstress Rita Navarro makes a quinceañera dress for Stefanie, she becomes involved with the girl's family and is attracted to her uncle.
Américas Commended 1995

Sweet, Sweet Fig Banana by Phillis Gershator. Fritz Millevoix, ill. A. Whitman, 1996. oop. na/K-3
Soto takes bananas he has grown to share with his friends at Market Square where his mother works.
Américas Commended 1996

Sweet Whispers, Brother Rush by Virginia Hamilton. Philomel, 1982. 3.8/3-6, 8.0/7-12
Tree is resentful of being left in charge of a retarded brother but encounters her uncle's ghost and comes to understand her family's problems.
Coretta Scott King Winner, Author 1983

Sworn Enemies by Carol Matas. Bantam, 1993. oop. na/5-9
In nineteenth-century Russia, Aaron is betrayed by a fellow Jew, taken by officers of the Czar, and forced into military service.
Sydney Taylor Winner, Older 1993

The Tale of Rabbit and Coyote by Tony Johnson. Tomie De Paola, ill. G. P. Putnam's Sons, 1994. 3.2/K-3
A Zapotec tale explaining why coyotes howl at the moon.
Américas Commended 1994

The Tales of Uncle Remus: The Adventures of Brer Rabbit by Julius Lester. Jerry Pinkney, ill. Dial, 1987. 3.0/3-6, 4.0/3-6
Afro-American tales about the adventures and misadventures of Brer Rabbit and his friends and enemies.
Coretta Scott King Honor, Author 1988

Talkin' About Bessie: The Story of Aviator Elizabeth Coleman by Nikki Grimes. Joseph Lorusso, ill. Orchard, 1998. 6.1/5-8
Biography of the first licensed Afro-American pilot.
Coretta Scott King Honor, Author 2003   Coretta Scott King Honor, Illustrator 2003

The Talking Eggs: A Folktale from the American South by Robert D. San Souci. Jerry Pinkney, ill. Dial, 1989. 4.4/K-3
Blanche follows the instructions of a witch and gains riches while her greedy sister makes fun of the old woman and is duly rewarded.
Coretta Scott King Honor, Illustrator 1990

The Tangerine Tree by Regina Hanson. Harvey Stevenson, ill. Clarion, 1995. 1.0/K-3
When Papa announces that he must leave Jamaica to work in America, Ida is heartbroken until he tells her a secret.
Américas Commended 1995

Tanuki's Gift by Tim Myer. Robert Roth, ill. Marshall Cavendish, 2003. 3.9/P-3, 3.9/K-3
One winter a priest takes in a furry tanuki and the two become friends, but when the tanuki tries to repay the priest, they both learn a lesson.
Asian Pacific American Honor, Illustration 2004

Tap-Tap by Karen Lynn Williams. Catherine Stock, ill. Clarion Books, 1994. 2.0/K-3
A Haitian mother and daughter sell oranges in the market to ride a passenger truck.
Américas Commended 1994

Tar Beach by Faith Ringgold. Crown, 1991. 2.0/K-3, 3.4/P-2
A girl dreams of flying above her Harlem home, claiming all she sees for herself and her family.
Coretta Scott King Winner, Illustrator 1992

Tatan'ka Iyota'ke: Sitting Bull and His World by Albert Marrin. Dutton, 2000. 7.8/6-12
Life of a Hunkpapa chief remembered for his defeat of General Custer at Little Big Horn.
Carter G. Woodson Winner, Secondary 2001

Teammates by Peter Golenback. Paul Bacon, ill. Harcourt, 1990. oop. na/ya
Describes prejudice experienced by Jackie Robinson when he joined the Brooklyn Dodgers and became the first black player in Major League baseball.
Carter G. Woodson Outstanding Merit, Elementary 1991

A Thief in the Village, and Other Stories by James Berry. Orchard, 1987. Puffin, 1990. 3.0/3-6
Stories about life in contemporary Jamaica, covering such subjects as a boy's desire to buy shoes and a girl's adventures on a coconut plantation.
Coretta Scott King Honor, Author 1989

This Life by Sidney Portier. Knopf, 1980. oop. na/ya
Autobiography of a trailblazing black actor.
Coretta Scott King Winner, Author 1981

This Strange New Feeling by Julius Lester. Dial, 1982. oop. na/ya
Three short stories about slavery and freedom in the South before the Civil War.
Coretta Scott King Honor, Author 1983

The Three Pigs: Nacho, Tito, and Miguel by Bobbi Salinas-Norman. Piñata Publications, 1998. 2.0/P-3
A contemporary, Mexican-American version of the three pigs story set in the Southwest.
Tomás Rivera Winner 1998

Through My Eyes by Ruby Bridges. Scholastic, 1999. 2.0/K-3
Bridges recounts the story of her involvement, as a six-year-old, in the integration of a school in New Orleans in 1960.
Carter G. Woodson Winner, Elementary 2000

Thunder Rose by Jerdine Nolen. Kadir Nelson, ill. Silver Whistle/Harcourt, 2003. 5.4/K-3
Thunder Rose performs amazing feats including building fences, taming a stampeding herd of steers, capturing rustlers, and turning aside a tornado.
Coretta Scott King Honor, Illustrator 2004

Thurgood Marshall: A Life for Justice by James Haskins. Henry Holt, 1992. oop. na/ya
Life and accomplishments of the first black judge appointed to the Supreme Court.
Carter G. Woodson Outstanding Merit, Secondary 1993

Till Victory Is Won: Black Soldiers in the Civil War by Zak Mettger. Lodestar, 1994. oop. na/ya
History of black soldiers involved in the Civil War.
Carter G. Woodson Winner, Secondary 1995

Tío Armando by Florence Parry Heide and Roxanne Heide Pierce. Ann Grifalconi, ill. Lothrop, Lee & Shepard, 1998. oop. na/1-3
Lucita's great-uncle Armando comes to live with them and teaches her many truths about life.
Américas Commended 1998

To Live in Two Worlds—American Indian Youth Today by Brent Ashabranner. Paul Conklin, ill. Dodd, Mead, 1984. oop. na/ya
Efforts of North American Indians to survive in and adjust to modern society while holding on to their ethnic heritage.
Carter G. Woodson Winner 1985

Tomás and the Library Lady by Pat Mora. Raul Colón, ill. Amy Prince, trans. Knopf, 1997. 2.0/K-3, 2.7/K-3
While helping his family of migrant laborers far from home, Tomás finds a world to explore in books at the public library.
Américas Commended 1997   Tomás Rivera Winner 1997

Tonight, by Sea by Frances Temple. Orchard, 1995. 5.0/3-6, 8.0/7-12
As governmental brutality become unbearable, Paulie joins others in
her Haitian village to help her uncle build a boat to escape to the U.S.
Américas Winner 1995

Toning the Sweep by Angela Johnson. Orchard, 1993. 4.7/5-8
On a visit to her grandmother Ola, who is dying of cancer, Emmie
hears stories about the past and her family history.
Coretta Scott King Winner, Author 1994

Tonio's Cat by Mary Calhoun. Edward Martínez, ill. Morrow, 1996.
oop. na/K-3
Toughy the cat helps fill the emptiness Tonio feels because he had to
leave his dog in Mexico.
Américas Commended 1996

The Tortilla Factory by Gary Paulsen. Ruth Wright Paulsen, ill.
Harcourt, 1995. 3.0/K-3, 4.0/3-6
A simple prose poem about how corn is harvested and made into
tortillas.
Américas Commended 1995

*Tough Questions Jews Ask: A Young Adult's Guide to Building a Jewish
Life* by Edward Feinstein. Jewish Lights Publishing, 2003. na/7-10
A conservative rabbi discusses Jewish commitment to spiritual
development.
Sydney Taylor Honor, Older 2003

Toussaint L'Ouverture: The Fight for Haiti's Freedom by Walter Dean
Myers. Jacob Lawrence, ill. Simon & Schuster, 1996. 5.0/3-6
Paintings by Jacob Lawrence chronicling the liberation of Haiti in 1804
under the leadership of General Toussaint L'Ouverture.
Américas Commended 1996

*The Tree Is Older Than You Are: A Bilingual Gathering of Poems and
Stories from Mexico with Paintings by Mexican Artists* selected by
Naomi Shihab Nye. Simon & Schuster, 1995. 4.0/3-6
Prose, poetry, and paintings about Mexico.
Américas Commended 1995

The Tree That Rains: The Flood Myth of the Huichol Indians of Mexico by Emery Bernhard and Durga Bernhard. Holiday House, 1994. oop. na/K-3
Watakame survives a great flood and begins a new life with the help of Great-Grandmother Earth.
Américas Commended 1994

The Trip Back Home by Janet S. Wong. Bo Jia, ill. Harcourt, 2000. 4.5/K-3
A girl and her mother travel to Korea to visit their extended family.
Asian Pacific American Winner 2000

The Trouble They Seen: Black People Tell the Story of Reconstruction edited by Dorothy Sterling. Doubleday, 1976. oop. na/ya
Lives of African Americans after the Civil War.
Carter G. Woodson Winner 1977

Trouble's Child by Mildred Pitts Walter. Lothrop, 1985. oop. na/6-10
Martha longs to leave her island home to go to high school and learn more than the ways of her midwife grandmother and someday broaden the lives of the villagers.
Coretta Scott King Honor, Author 1986

Tukama Tootles the Flute: A Tale from the Antilles by Phillis Gershator. Synthia Saint James, ill. Orchard Books, 1994. 2.0/K-3
Tukama is captured by a two-headed giant and held prisoner but uses his flute to escape.
Américas Commended 1994

The Tuskegee Airmen: Black Heroes of World War II by Jacqueline Harris. Dillon, 1996. oop. na/6-9
African-American pilots in World War II.
Carter G. Woodson Honor, Secondary 1997

Two Days in May by Harriet Peck Taylor. Leyla Torres, ill. Farrar, Straus & Giroux, 1999. 3.4/K-3
Neighbors join together to help five deer who wander into the city in search of food.
Américas Commended 1999

Uncle Jed's Barbershop by Margaree King Mitchell. James Ransome, ill. Simon & Schuster, 1993. 3.8/P-3
Despite obstacles and setbacks, Sarah Jean's Uncle Jed, the only black barber in the county, pursues a dream of opening his own barbershop.
Coretta Scott King Honor, Illustrator 1994

Uncle Misha's Partisans by Yuri Suhl. Four Winds, 1973. Shapolsky Publishers, 1988. oop. na/ya
During World War II in the Ukraine, an orphaned Jewish boy joins a band of partisans who give him an important assignment against the Nazis.
Sydney Taylor Winner 1973

Uncle Rain Cloud by Tony Johnson. Fabricio Vanden Broeck, ill. Charlesbridge, 2001. 2.0/K-3, 3.1/3-6
Carlos tries to help his uncle, who is frustrated at his inability to speak English, adjust to their new home in Los Angeles.
Américas Commended 2001

Uncle Snake by Matthew Gollub. Leovigildo Martínez, ill. Tambourine, 1996. 3.9/K-3
When his face is changed into that of a snake after he visits a forbidden cave, a boy wears a mask for twenty years before being taken into the sky.
Américas Commended 1996

Under the Royal Palms: A Childhood in Cuba by Alma Flor Ada. Atheneum, 1998. 6.6/3-6
Author recalls growing up in Cuba.
Américas Commended 1998   Pura Belpré Winner, Narrative 2000

Under the Sunday Tree by Eloise Greenfield. Amos Ferguson, ill. Harper, 1988. 4.0/3-6
Poems and paintings evoke life in the Bahamas.
Coretta Scott King Honor, Illustrator 1989

The Uninvited Guest and Other Jewish Holiday Tales by Nina Jaffe. Elivia Savadier, ill. Scholastic, 1993. oop. na/K-6
Background information and retellings of traditional Jewish tales related to major holidays such as Yom Kippur, Sukkot, Hanukkah, and Purim.
Sydney Taylor Winner, Younger 1993

Uptown by Bryan Collier. Henry Holt, 2000. 2.0/K-3, 2.8/K-3
A tour of the sights of Harlem, including brownstones, shopping on 125th Street, a barber shop, summer basketball, the Boy's Choir, and sunset over the Harlem River.
Coretta Scott King Winner, Illustrator 2001

Vejigantes Masquerader by Lulu Delacre. Scholastic, 1993. na/1-4
Against all odds, a resourceful Puerto Rican boy manages to get a costume for Carnival.
Américas Winner 1993

Vilma Martínez by Corrin Codye. Susi Kilgore, ill. Raintree Publications, 1990. oop. na/4-6
Biography of a lawyer who won many landmark civil rights cases.
Carter G. Woodson Outstanding Merit, Elementary 1990

Virgie Goes to School with Us Boys by Elizabeth Fitzgerald Howard. E. B. Lewis, ill. Simon & Schuster, 1999. 2.5/K-3
In the post-Civil War South, an African-American girl is determined to go to school just like her older brothers.
Coretta Scott King Honor, Illustrator 2001

Visiting Langston by Willie Perdomo. Bryan Collier, ill. Henry Holt, 2002. 1.6/3-6
Poem celebrating the African-American poet Langston Hughes.
Coretta Scott King Honor, Illustrator 2003

Voices from the Fields: Children of Migrant Farmworkers Tell Their Stories. Interviews and photographs by S. Beth Atkin. Little, Brown, 1993. 6.0/5-8
Photographs, poems, and interviews reveal the hardships and hopes of Mexican-American migrant farmworkers and their families.
Américas Commended 1994

W. E. B. Dubois by Patricia C. McKissack and Fredrick L. McKissack. Franklin Watts, 1990. oop. na/5-9
Examines the upbringing, education, writings, and political activities of a founder of the NAACP.
Carter G. Woodson Outstanding Merit, Secondary 1991

Waiting for Mama by Marietta Moskin. Richard Lebenson, ill. Coward, McCann & Geoghegan, 1975. oop. na/4-6
A Russian immigrant family living in New York in the early 1900s prepares for the long-awaited arrival of their mother and baby sister.
Sydney Taylor Winner 1975

Walking Stars: Stories of Magic and Power by Victor Villaseñor. Piñata Books, 1994. 5.6/5-8, 8.0/7-12
Autobiographical stories about growing up as the son of Mexican immigrants in California.
Américas Commended 1994

Walking the Road to Freedom: A Story about Sojourner Truth by Jeri Ferris. Peter E. Hanson, ill. Carolrhoda Books, 1988. 5.9/3-6
Life of a black woman orator who spoke out against slavery in New England and the Midwest.
Carter G. Woodson Winner 1989

War Cry on a Prayer Feather: Prose and Poetry of the Ute by Nancy Wood. Doubleday, 1979. oop. na/ya
Poetry of the Ute Indians.
Carter G. Woodson Winner 1980

The Watsons Go to Birmingham—1963 by Christopher Paul Curtis. Delacorte, 1995. Holt, Rinehart & Winston, 1995. Thorndike Press, 2000. 4.0/3-6, 5.0/5-8, 6.0/5-8
Lives of the Watsons, an African-American family in Michigan, are drastically changed after they go to visit Grandma in Alabama in 1963.
Coretta Scott King Honor, Author 1996

What a Morning! The Christmas Story in Black Spirituals selected by John Langstaff. Ashley Bryan, ill. Macmillan, 1987. oop. na/2-6
Five illustrated spirituals dealing with the birth of Christ.
Coretta Scott King Honor, Illustrator 1988

What I Had Was Singing: The Story of Marian Anderson by Jeri Ferris. Carolrhoda Books, 1994. 6.5/5-8
Biography of the African-American singer who performed at the Lincoln Memorial and the Metropolitan Opera in the 1950s.
Carter G. Woodson Winner, Elementary 1995

When I Am Old With You by Angela Johnson. David Soman, ill. Orchard, 1990. 2.7/K-3
A child imagines being old with Grandaddy and joining him in playing cards all day, visiting the ocean, and eating bacon on the porch.
Coretta Scott King Honor, Author 1991

When I Left My Village by Maxine Rose Schur. Brian Pinkney, ill. Dial, 1996. oop. na/3-6
An Ethiopian Jewish family leaves their oppressed mountain village to make a difficult journey in the hope of reaching freedom in Israel.
Sydney Taylor Winner, Older 1996

When Jaguars Ate the Moon and Other Stories about Animals and Plants of the Americas by María Cristina Brusca and Toña Wilson. Henry Holt, 1995. oop. na/1-4
Folktales from the Americas.
Américas Commended 1995

When the Beginning Began: Stories about God, the Creatures, and Us by Julius Lester. Emily Lisker, ill. Harcourt, 1999. 6.0/5-8
Traditional and original Jewish tales interpreting the Biblical story of creation.
Sydney Taylor Honor, Older 1999

When the Chickens Went on Strike: A Rosh Hashanah Tale by Erica Silverman. Matthew Trueman, ill. Dutton, 2003. 2.7/2-4
A Jewish boy in Russia learns a lesson from the village chickens.
Sydney Taylor Honor, Younger 2003

When the Monkeys Came Back by Kristine L. Franklin. Robert Roth, ill. Atheneum, 1994. oop. 2.0/K-3
Marta plants trees in her Costa Rican village to bring the monkeys back.
Américas Commended 1994

When the Soldiers Were Gone by Vera W. Propp. Putnam, 1999. 3.5/3-6
After German occupation of the Netherlands, Benjamin leaves the Christian family with whom he had been living and reunites with his parents.
Sydney Taylor Honor, Older 1999

When Zaydeh Danced on Eldridge Street by Elsa Okon Rael. Marjorie Priceman, ill. Simon & Schuster, 1997. oop. na/K-3
While staying with her grandparents in New York in the mid-1930s, Zeesie joins in the celebration of Simchat Torah and sees a different side of her stern grandfather.
Sydney Taylor Winner, Younger 1997

Where Fireflies Dance/Ahí, donde bailan las luciérnagas by Lucha Corpi. Mira Reisberg, ill. Children's Book Press, 1997. 2.0/K-3
A girl and her brother spend their childhood in a town on the Caribbean coast of Mexico.
Américas Commended 1997

Where the Flame Trees Bloom by Alma Flor Ada. Antonio Martorell, ill. Atheneum, 1994. 6.1/3-6
Stories about relatives and friends that were part of the author's childhood in Cuba.
Américas Commended 1994

Which Way Freedom? by Joyce Hansen. Walker, 1986. 4.5/3-6
Obi escapes from slavery during the Civil War, joins a black Union regiment, and becomes involved in the fighting in Tennessee.
Coretta Scott King Honor, Author 1987

White Bread Competition by Jo Ann Yolanda Hernández. Piñata Books, 1997. 6.0/5-8
When Luz, a ninth-grade student, is the first Latina to win a spelling competition, her success triggers a variety of emotions among family, friends, and the community.
Américas Commended 1997

Who Was the Woman Who Wore the Hat? by Nancy Patz. Dutton Books, 2003. 3.0/3-6
Meditation on a woman's hat on display in the Jewish Historical Museum in Amsterdam.
Sydney Taylor Winner, Older 2003

The Wisdom Bird: A Tale of Solomon and Sheba by Sheldon Oberman. Neil Waldman, ill. Boyds Mills Press, 2000. 2.0/K-3, 3.7/3-6
Solomon and Sheba learn that it is better to break a promise than do something wrong.
Sydney Taylor Honor, Younger 2000

Women of Hope: African Americans Who Made a Difference by Joyce Hansen. Scholastic, 1998. 7.8/4-10
Photographs and biographies of thirteen African-American women.
Carter G. Woodson Honor, Secondary 1999

The Words of Martin Luther King, Jr. compiled by Coretta Scott King. Newmarket Press, 1983. 7.0/7-12
Quotations on many subjects including civil rights, racism, justice, and more.
Coretta Scott King, Special Citation

Working Cotton by Sherley Anne William. Carole Byard, ill. Harcourt, 1992. 2.0/K-3, 3.9/P-2
A black girl relates events of her family's migrant life in the cotton fields of California.
Coretta Scott King Honor, Illustrator 1993

Xochitl and the Flowers/ Xóchitl, la niña de las flores by Jorge Argueta. Carl Angel, ill. Children's Book Press, 2003. 2.0/K-3
Xochitl and her family, newly arrived from El Salvador, create a plant nursery in place of the garbage heap behind their apartment and celebrate with friends and neighbors.
Américas Commended 2003

The Year by Suzanne Lange. S. G. Phillips, 1970. oop. na/7-9
Life on an Israeli Kibbutz.
Sydney Taylor Winner 1970

The Year They Walked: Rosa Parks and the Montgomery Bus Boycott by Beatrice Siegel. Four Winds, 1992. 7.3/3-6
Life of Rosa Parks and her role in the Montgomery bus boycott.
Carter G. Woodson Outstanding Merit, Secondary 1993

You May Plow Here: The Narrative of Sara Brooks edited by Thordis Simonsen. Norton, 1986. Simon and Schuster, 1987. oop. na/ya
Oral history of a black domestic worker beginning with her childhood on a farm in Alabama and continuing through thirty years of domestic service in Cleveland.
Carter G. Woodson Outstanding Merit 1988

The Young Landlords by Walter Dean Myers. Viking, 1979. Puffin, 1989. 5.1/7-12
Five friends become landlords and try to make their Harlem neighborhood a better place.
Coretta Scott King Winner, Author 1980

Yussel's Prayer by Barbara Cohen. Michael J. Deraney, ill. Lothrop, Lee & Shepard, 1981. oop. na/K-3
A cowherd's simple, sincere Yom Kippur prayer is instrumental in ending the day's fast.
Sydney Taylor Winner, Younger 1981

SUBJECT INDEX

Escape to Freedom

Freedom River

Gwendolyn Brooks

Her Stories

I Am Rosa Parks

I Never Had It Made

James Van DerZee

Langston Hughes

Lena Horne

Leon's Story

Let It Shine!

Madam C. J. Walker

Make a Joyful Noise . . .

Malcolm X

Marian Anderson

Martin Luther King, Jr. . . .

Martin's Big Words

Mary: An Autobiography

Mary McLeod Bethune

Master of Mahogany

Matthew Henson

Maya Angelou

Minty

Movin' Up

Only Passing Through

Outward Dreams

Paul Robeson, Hero . . .

Portia

Pride Against Prejudice

Princess of the Press

Rap a Tap Tap

Ray Charles

Red-Tail Angels

The Riches of Oseola . . .

Rosa Parks

Seventeen Black Artists

Shirley Chisholm, Teacher . . .

Slavery Time When I Was . . .

Sojourner Truth: Ain't . . .

Sojourner Truth: From . . .

Sorrow's Kitchen

Soul Looks Back in Wonder

Starting Home

The Story of Stevie Wonder

Story Painter

Strong Right Arm

Talkin' About Bessie

Teammates

This Life

Through My Eyes

Thurgood Marshall

The Tuskegee Airmen

W. E. B. Dubois

Walking the Road to . . .

What I Had Was Singing

Women of Hope

The Words of Martin . . .

The Year They Walked

You May Plow Here

African Americans—Fiction

Almost to Freedom

The Bat Boy & His Violin

Because We Are

The Bell of Christmas

Bright Shadow

Bronx Masquerade

Bud, Not Buddy

C.L.O.U.D.S

The Captive

Circle of Gold

Cornrows

The Dark-Thirty

An Enchanted Hair Tale

Everett Anderson's Goodbye

Fallen Angels

The First Part Last

Forged by Fire

Brothers
The Color of My Words
Coolies
Forged by Fire
Justice and Her Brothers
Locomotion
Miracle's Boys
Miro in the Kingdom . . .
Motown and Didi
My Very Own Room
The Secret of Two Brothers
The Singing Man
Sweet Whispers, Brother Rush
Virgie Goes to School . . .
The Watsons Go to . . .
Where Fireflies Dance

Buddhism
Tanuki's Gift

Buffalo
Buffalo Days
Buffalo Hunt

Burns, Anthony, 1834-1862
Anthony Burns

Butterflies
Butterfly Boy

C

California
The Afterlife
Angels Ride Bikes . . .
Barrio
Baseball in April . . .
Breaking Through
Buried Onions
Calling the Doves
Celebrating Chinese New . . .
Celebrating Hanukkah
César Chávez
Dragonwings

Esperanza Rising
First Day in Grapes
Grandma and Me at the Flea
Harvesting Hope
Hoang Anh
Konnichiwa!
Lolo & Red Legs
A Movie in My Pillow
Petty Crimes
The Red Rose Box
The Stowaway
Summer on Wheels
Uncle Rain Cloud
Walking Stars
Working Cotton
Xochitl and the Flowers

Cancer
A Sunburned Prayer
Toning the Sweep

Caribbean Area
Before We Were Free
Behind the Mountains
Caribbean Alphabet
A Caribbean Counting Book
A Caribbean Dozen
Caribbean Dream
Cendrillon
Cocoa Ice
The Color of My Words
The Crab Man
La Cucaracha Martina
Darkfright
Doctor Bird
Down by the River
The Face at the Window
Feliz Nochebuena, Feliz . . .
Firefly Summer
For the Life of Laetitia
Fruits

Born Confused
Bronx Masquerade
Brown Honey in . . .
Duey's Tale
Multiethnic Teens and . . .
Illinois
   Celebrating Kwanzaa
   Gwendolyn Brooks
Imagination
   Daydreamers
   Dragonwings
   Hooray, a Piñata!
   Isla
   Outward Dreams
   Tar Beach
   When I Am Old With You
Immigrants (U.S.)
   Atlas of Asian-American . . .
   Children of the Maya
   The Chinese Americans
   Coming to North America . . .
   Hector Lives in the United . . .
   I Am of Two Places
   Into a Strange Land
   A Movie in My Pillow
   My Two Worlds
   New Kids on the Block
   Over Here It's Different
Immigrants—Fiction
   The Always Prayer Shawl
   Behind the Mountains
   Beyond the High White Wall
   Call Me Ruth
   The Castle on Hester Street
   Chanukah on the Prairie
   Coolies
   Dear Abuelita
   Elena
   Esperanza Rising

Flight to Freedom
Going Home
The Keeping Quilt
Letters from Rifka
My Diary from Here to There
A Picture of Grandmother
Rivka's First Thanksgiving
A Russian Farewell
A Step from Heaven
The Tangerine Tree
Tonight, by Sea
Tonio's Cat
The Trip Back Home
Uncle Rain Cloud
Waiting for Mama
Walking Stars
Xochitl and the Flowers
Incas
   Miro in the Kingdom . . .
Incest
   I Hadn't Meant to . . .
India and Indian Americans (U.S.)
   Atlas of Asian-American . . .
   Born Confused
Indians of Central America
   Children of the Maya
   Imagining Isabel
   The Invisible Hunters
   Journey of the Nightly Jaguar
   People of Corn
Indians of Mexico
   Angela Weaves a Dream
   La Boda
   Cuckoo
   Heart of a Jaguar
   How Music Came . . .
   The Journey of Tunuri . . .
   Mayeros
   The Sad Night

Japanese Americans
  Atlas of Asian-American . . .
  Daniel Inouye
  The Japanese American . . .
  Konnichiwa!
Japanese Americans—Fiction
  Beacon Hill Boys
Japanese Americans—Relocation
(WWII)
  Children of the Relocation . . .
  The Children of Topaz
  A Fence Away from Freedom
  In America's Shadow
  Life in a Japanese . . .
  Remembering Manzanar
Jazz
  Black Music in America
  Don't Explain
  Duke Ellington
  Ella Fitzgerald
  The Sound That Jazz Makes
Jewish Historical Museum
  Who Was the Woman . . .
Jews—Biography
  The Endless Steppe
  In the Mouth of the Wolf
  Shalom, Haver
  Sigmund Freud
Jews—Fiction
  The Always Prayer Shawl
  Bagels from Benny
  Berchick
  Beyond the High White Wall
  Birdland
  Cakes and Miracles
  Call Me Ruth
  The Castle on Hester Street
  Chanukah on the Prairie
  Chicken Soup by Heart

A Cloak for the Moon
Daddy's Chair
Dancing on the Bridge . . .
The Devil in Vienna
The Devil's Arithmetic
Exit from Home
Ike and Mama and the . . .
The Island on Bird Street
The Keeping Quilt
The Key Is Lost
Letters from Rifka
Love You, Soldier
The Market Wedding
Mrs. Moskowitz and . . .
The Night Journey
Number the Stars
Our Eddie
Pearl's Passover
The Peddler's Gift
A Picture of Grandmother
The Return
Rivka's First Thanksgiving
A Russian Farewell
Speed of Light
Star of Fear, Star of Hope
Stones in Water
Sworn Enemies
Uncle Misha's Partisans
When I Left My Village
When the Chickens Went . . .
When the Soldiers Were Gone
When Zaydeh Danced
Jews—Folklore
  The Diamond Tree
  Gershon's Monster
  Joseph Had a Little Overcoat
  Joseph Who Loved . . .
  Journeys with Elijah
  My Grandmother's Stories

César Chávez
 The Christmas Gift
 The Circuit
 Dark Harvest
 First Day in Grapes
 Gathering the Sun
 Going Home
 Harvest
 Harvesting Hope
 Lights on the River
 La Mariposa
 Radio Man
 Tomás and the Library Lady
 Voices from the Fields
 Working Cotton
Miskito Indians
 The Invisible Hunters
Mississippi
 The Friendship
 Let the Circle Be Unbroken
 The "Mississippi Burning". . .
 Mississippi Challenge
 The Riches of Oseola . . .
 The Road to Memphis
Mistakes
 The Chanukkah Guest
 The Old Man and His Door
Mixed Ethnicity/Heritage
 All the Colors of the Race
 Edmonia Lewis
 I Love Saturdays y Domingos
 Jalapeño Bagels
 The Land
 Liliana's Grandmothers
 Living in Two Worlds
 Miracle's Boys
 Multiethnic Teens and . . .
Money
 Circle of Gold

 Money-Hungry
 My Rows and Piles of Coins
 Pedrito's Day
Monkeys
 Pascual's Magic Pictures
 When the Monkeys
Montana
 Buffalo Days
 Morning Star . . .
Montezuma
 The Sad Night
Moon
 Big Moon Tortilla
 A Cloak for the Moon
 From the Bellybutton . . .
 Half a Moon and One . . .
 When Jaguars Ate the Moon
Moses (Biblical Leader)
 The Moses Basket
Mothers
 All the Colors of the Race
 Berchick
 Cakes and Miracles
 Call Me Ruth
 Childtimes
 Circle of Gold
 CrashBoomLove
 Duey's Tale
 Elena
 Erandi's Braids
 Esperanza Rising
 From the Notebooks . . .
 Heaven
 Hi!
 Ike and Mama and the . . .
 Juan Bobo Goes to Work
 The Land
 Let the Lion Eat Straw
 Little Eight John

Mama Does the Mambo

Miracle's Boys

Money-Hungry

Mother Crocodile

My Mama Needs Me

The Patchwork Quilt

Pedrito's Day

A Picture of Grandmother

Prietita and the Ghost . . .

Rainbow Jordan

A Step from Heaven

Sweet, Sweet Fig Banana

Tap-Tap

The Trip Back Home

Waiting for Mama

Moving, Household

The Christmas Gift

The Circuit

First Day in Grapes

Grandmama's Joy

Hector Lives in the United . . .

Mrs. Moskowitz and . . .

My Diary from Here to There

Murder

The Afterlife

Beyond the High White Wall

Francie

Monster

Music and Musicians

Aïda

All Night, All Day

The Bat Boy & His Violin

Black Music in America

Calling the Doves

Caribbean Alphabet

A Caribbean Counting Book

Christmas in the Big . . .

A Cry from the Earth

Diez Deditos

Don't Explain

Down by the River

Duke Ellington

Ella Fitzgerald

How Music Came . . .

i see the rhythm

I'm Going to Sing

Island in the Sun

Lena Horne

Make a Joyful Noise . . .

Marian Anderson

Movin' Up

Paul Robeson, Hero . . .

Pearl's Passover

Ray Charles

The Singing Man

The Sound That Jazz Makes

The Story of Stevie Wonder

Tukama Tootles the Flute

What a Morning!

What I Had Was Singing

Where Fireflies Dance

Women of Hope

Mustaches

Big Bushy Mustache

N

Nature

Alejandro's Gift

Caribbean Alphabet

Cool Melons—Turn to Frogs!

Fernando's Gift

From the Bellybutton . . .

Gathering the Sun

The Hunterman and . . .

Laughing Tomatoes . . .

The Magical Maguey

Morning Star

Navajo Indians

Noah's Ark
Noise
　La Cucaracha Martina
North Carolina
　Leon's Story
North Dakota
　Chanukah on the Prairie
North Pole
　Arctic Explorer
　Matthew Henson
Numbers
　A Caribbean Counting Book
　Count on Your Fingers . . .
　Diez Deditos
　Fruits
　Josefina
　Just a Minute
　Nine Spoons
　The Number on My . . .
Nuns
　A Library for Juana
Nursery Rhymes
　A Caribbean Counting Book
　Diez Deditos
　Down by the River
　Grandmother's Nursery . . .

O

Oasis
　Alejandro's Gift
Ogibwa Indians
　Edmonia Lewis
Oglala Indians
　The Life and Death of . . .
Ohio
　The Bells of Christmas
　Freedom River
　You May Plow Here
Oklahoma

Bright Shadow
　I Have Heard of a Land
Old Age
　Junius Over Far
　When I am Old With You
Omaha Indians
　Native American Doctor
Opera
　Aïda
　What I Had Was Singing
Orphans
　Asphalt Angels
　Bud, Not Buddy
　I'm José and I'm Okay
　Locomotion
　Miracle's Boys
　A Single Shard

P

Painters and Painting
　Family Pictures
　Fireflies in the Dark
　Frida
　The Great Migration
　In My Family
　The Little Painter of . . .
　Murals
　My Mexico
　Starting Home
　Story Painter
　The Tree Is Older . . .
　Under the Sunday Tree
Palestine
　Ancient Israelites and . . .
Panama
　Beyond the Ancient Cities
　The Little Painter of . . .
　Marisol and Magdalena
Parker, John P., 1827-1900

The Keeping Quilt
The Patchwork Quilt
Quinceañera
   Cuba 15
   Sweet Fifteen

R

Rabbits
   The Days When the . . .
   Nina Bonita
   Rabbit Wishes
   The Tales of Uncle Remus
Rabin, Yitzhak, 1922-1995
   Shalom, Haver
Radio
   Radio Man
Railroads
   The Chinese Americans
   Coolies
   A Long Hard Journey
Rain Forests
   Fernando's Gift
Ramadan
   Ramadan
Ranch Life
   Chave's Memories
   In the Days of the Vaqueros
   Justin and the Best . . .
Recipes
   Christmas in the Big . . .
   Pearl's Passover
   Salsa Stories
Recycling
   Joseph Had a Little Overcoat
   Something from Nothing
Reese, Pee Wee, 1919-1999
   Teammates
Refugees
   Children of the Maya

Into a Strange Land
   Tonight, by Sea
Relocation Camps (U.S. Japanese)
   See Japanese Americans—Relocation
Responsibility
   Pedrito's Day
   Sweet Whispers, Brother Rush
Reynoso, Anthony
   Anthony Reynoso
Rivers
   Down by the River
   Freedom River
   Lights on the River
   Ransom for a River Dolphin
   Uptown
Roadrunner
   Roadrunner's Dance
Robeson, Paul, 1898-1976
   Paul Robeson, Hero . . .
Robinson, Bill, 1878-1949
   Rap a Tap Tap
Robinson, Jackie, 1919-1972
   Early Black Reformers
   I Never Had It Made
   Teammates
Rodeo
   Anthony Reynoso
Rodríguez, Kirsy
   My Two Worlds
Roessel, Jaclyn
   Songs from the Loom
Roping
   Anthony Reynoso
Rosh Hashanah
   When the Chickens Went . . .
Runaways
   Bud, Not Buddy
   The Daring Escape . . .
   The Red Comb

AUTHORS, EDITORS, ILLUSTRATORS, AND TRANSLATORS INDEX

Bertrand, Diane Gonzáles 90
Bierhorst, John 26
Binch, Caroline 30, 43
Blanc, Esther Silverstein 12
Blanco, Alberto 7
Blanco, Osvaldo J. 34
Bloom, Valerie 37
Bode, Janet 70
Boeke, Wanda 9
Bootman, Colin 6
Boyd, Candy Dawson 23
Bridges, Ruby 92, 109
Broeck, Fabricio Vanden 96
Broida, Marian 7
Brown, David Scott 12
Brown, Tricia 53
Brusca, María Cristina 75, 99
Bryan, Ashley 6, 8, 11, 46, 56, 99
Bryant, Michael 58
Buffalohead, Julie 82
Bullar, Pamela 41
Bunting, Eve 38, 72
Burgess, Lord 49
Butler, Mary G. 86
Byard, Carole 5, 26, 39, 101

C

Caines, Jeanette 52
Calhoun, Mary 94
Capellinni, Mary 44, 88
Carden, Mary 44
Carling, Amelia Lau 60
Carlson, Lori M. 10, 25
Carmi, Giora 21
Carver, Susan 24
Casilla, Robert 35, 50, 57
Castañeda, Omar S. 5, 47
Castillo, Ana 67
Cepeda, Joe 13, 51, 72

Chambers, Veronica 61
Chapman, Robert 38
Charles, Faustin 18
Chilcoat, George W. 23
Childress, Alice 78
Chin-Lee, Cynthia 5
Chodos-Irvine, Margaret 8
Christie, Gregory 72, 74
Ciavonne, Jean 19
Clair, Donna 19
Clay, Wil 44, 57
Clifton, Lucille 32
Coalson, Glo 42
Codye, Corrin 97
Cohen, Barbara 102
Coleman, Evelyn 80
Collier, Bryan 36, 61, 97
Colón, Raul 93
Comino, Sandra 56
Conklin, Paul 22, 28, 66, 93
Cooper, Floyd 16, 45, 63
Cooper, Martha 8, 68
Cooper, Michael L. 80
Córdova, Amy 68
Corpi, Lucha 100
Cotts, Claire B. 23
Cowley, Joy 13
Crespo, George 43
Cruz, Bárbara C. 67
Cruz López, Casimiro de la 51
Cummings, Pat 17, 52, 68, 88
Curtis, Christopher Paul 17, 98
Curtis, Gavin 10
Czernecki, Stefan 44

D

Danticat, Edwidge 12
Dávalos, Felipe 57, 83
Davis, Aubrey 9

Davis, Ossie 32
Davison, Patricia Hinton 19
Dawson, Mildred Leinweber 73
de la Peña, Terri 5
de López, Marianno 36
De Paola, Tomie 32, 54, 90
De Veaux, Alexis 30, 32
Delacre, Lulu 15, 38, 82, 83, 97
Delgado, María Isabel 22
DeLucio-Brock, Anita 39
Deraney, Michael J. 102
Desai Hidier, Tanuja 15
Diakité, Baba Wagué 44
Díaz, David 38, 76, 81
Díaz, Lidia 43
Dillon, Diane 6, 42, 60, 75, 79
Dillon, Leo 6, 42, 60, 75, 79
Diop, Birago 66
Dixon, Tennessee 12
Domínguez, Joseph F. 76
Dooling, Michael 56
Dorros, Arthur 48, 78
Dorros, Sandra Marulanda 48, 78
Dorsey, Bob 13
Dragonwagon, Crescent 40
Draper, Sharon M. 10, 36
Duckett, Alfred 45
Dugan, Karen 74
Duggleby, John 89

E

Echo-Hawk, Roger C. 10
Echo-Hawk, Walter R. 10
Edelstein, Terese 28, 53
Ehlert, Lois 27
Eichenbaum, Rose 71
Endredy, James 51
English, Karen 36, 69
Erdrich, Lise 82

F

Fagan, Cary 61
Faría, Rosana 70
Faulkner, William J. 29
Fax, Elton C. 83
Feelings, Tom 29, 64, 86, 87, 118
Feinstein, Edward 94
Felstead, Cathie 18
Fenner, Carol 85
Ferguson, Amos 96, 118
Ferrer, Ismael Espinosa 34
Ferris, Jeri 8, 69, 98, 99
Fincher, E. B. 64
Fireside, Harvey 65
Fisher, Leonard Everett 82
Flake, Sharon G. 65
Flournoy, Valerie 74
Fogelman, Phyllis 87
Forberg, Ati 85
Ford, George 79
Foxx, Jeffrey Jay 7
Frampton, David 65
Franklin, Kristine L. 100
Frasconi, Antonio 76
Freedman, Florence B. 16
Freedman, Russell 17, 47, 55
Friedman, Judith 9
Fuenmayor, Morella 87

G

Gage, Amy Glaser 74
Galindo, Mary Sue 46
Galvez, Daniel 49
Garay, Luis 49, 75
Garcia, Stephanie 85
Garland, Sherry 48
Garza, Carmen Lomas 33, 47, 59, 121
Geeslin, Campbell 47

Geras, Adèle 68
Gerber, Pesach 70
Gershator, David 40
Gershator, Phillis 40, 79, 90, 95
Gerson, Mary-Joan 43, 76
Gerstein, Mordicai 71
Ghazi, Suhaib Hamid 78
Gilchrist, Jan Spivey 69, 70
Gilman, Phoebe 86
Ginsburg, Max 36
Glass, Frankcina 62
Goldin, Barbara Diamond 17, 51
Golembe, Carla 43, 76
Golenback, Peter 92
Gollub, Matthew 25, 96
Gómez, Elizabeth 66
Gonzáles, Edward 33
González, Lucia M. 15, 83
González, Maya Christina 8, 37, 44, 46, 54, 67, 69, 77
González, Ralfka 68
González-Jensen, Margarita 64
Goodsell, Jane 28
Gordon, Ginger 8, 68
Gordy, Berry 66, 121
Grebu, Devis 50
Green, Michelle Y. 89
Greenfield, Eloise 5, 23, 29, 39, 62, 69, 70, 81, 96, 122
Gregory, Kristiana 89
Grifalconi, Ann 32, 93
Griffith, Gershom 88
Grimes, Nikki 16, 50, 63, 86, 91
Griswold del Castillo, Richard 21
Grossman, Patricia 82
Guevara, Susan 21, 67
Gunning, Monica 71
Gutiérrez, Rudy 72
Guy, Rosa 66

H

Haas, Shelly O. 27
Hall, Diane 20
Hallworth, Grace 30
Hamilton, Virginia 8, 12, 42, 52, 57, 59, 60, 75, 90
Hanna, Cheryl 32
Hansen, Joyce 15, 18, 45, 100, 101
Hanson, Peter E. 98
Hanson, Regina 33, 91
Harlan, Judith 7, 42
Harris, Jacqueline 95
Haskins, James 7, 9, 11, 14, 19, 41, 44, 50, 54, 60, 73, 89, 93
Hausman, Gerald 30
Hautzig, Esther 32, 76, 122
Hazelton, Hugh 49
Heide, Florence Parry 93
Heller, Linda 20
Hernández, Irene Beltrán 83
Hernández, Jo Ann Yolanda 101
Hernández de la Cruz, María 51
Herrera, Juan Felipe 18, 26, 39, 54, 123
Hershenhorn, Esther 22
Hesse, Karen 55
Hest, Amy 58
Hewett, Joan 42
Hewett, Richard 42
Heyman, Anita 33
Hinkle, Alice 77
Hirsch, Marilyn 50
Hirschfelder, Arlene B. 40
Hodge, Merle 35
Hoestlandt, Jo 88
Holtwijk, Ineke 9
Holzwarth, Werner 46
Hoobler, Dorothy 50
Hoobler, Thomas 50

Lester, Julius 90, 92, 99
Levine, Ellen 34
Levine, Karen 40
Levine, Melinda 39
Levitin, Sonia 80
Levy, Janice 87
Lewin, Ted 7
Lewis, E. B. 10, 68, 97
Linnea, Sharon 77
Lisandrelli, Elaine Slivinski 62
Lisker, Emily 99
Little, Lessie Jones 23, 128
Litwin, Laura Baskes 62
Litzinger, Rosanne 22
Livingston, Myra Cohn 76
Lizardi-Rivera, Carmen 65
Long, Sylvia 6
López, Loretta 14
Lorusso, Joseph 91
Lowry, Lois 72
Loya, Olga 65
Lucas, Cedric 26
Luenn, Nancy 38
Lurie, Leon 16
Lusebrink, Karen 39
Lyons, Mary E. 62, 87, 88

M

Machado, Ana María 63, 70
Mack, Tracy 13
Madrigal, Antonio Hernández 32
Mair, Jacqueline 44
Markun, Patricia Maloney 57
Marlow, Eric 81
Marrin, Albert 92
Martínez, Edward 94
Martínez, Floyd 88
Martínez, Leovigildo 96
Martínez, Victor 74

Martorell, Antonio 86, 100
Matas, Carol 90
Mathews, Sally Schofer 82
Mathis, Sharon Bell 79
McGowan, Gary 15
McGuire, Paula 24
McKenna, Laura 46
McKissack, Fredrick L. 14, 19, 23, 29, 58, 79, 80, 86, 98
McKissack, Patricia C. 14, 19, 23, 28, 29, 38, 58, 64, 79, 80, 86, 98
Meade, Holly 24, 79
Mebane, Mary E. 62, 129
Medearis, Angela Shelf 77, 84
Mellage, Nanette 24
Meltzer, Milton 23, 53, 70
Merino, Jose María 12
Merola, Caroline 63
Mettger, Zak 93
Meyer, Carolyn 80
Migdale, Lawrence 17, 20, 43, 77
Mike, Jan 51
Millevoix, Fritz 90
Minter, Daniel 80
Mitchell, Margaree King 96
Mitchell, Rita Phillips 43
Mlawer, Teresa 87
Mochizuki, Ken 11
Mohr, Nicholasa 72, 86
Mollel, Tololwa M. 68
Montes, Marisa 51
Moore, Cathy 28
Moore, Joseph 77
Mora, Pat 25, 55, 74, 93
Morales, Rodolfo 7
Morales, Yuyi 41, 52
Moretón, Daniel 27
Moskin, Marietta 98
Mugabane, Peter 14

ABOUT THE
AUTHOR

Sherry York worked as an educator in Texas from 1969 through 1999. During those years she was a teacher at middle schools, high schools, and colleges; a school librarian; a reading program supervisor; and board member of two public libraries. Since retirement York has written reviews and articles for *Library Talk*, *The Book Report*, *Library Media Connection*, *VOYA*, *Texas Books in Review*, *Southwestern American Literature*, *ALAN Review*, *Concho River Review*, and *New Mexico Journal of Reading*. The author of three previous Linworth books on minority-authored literature and an advocate of multicultural literature for young readers, she has presented programs at conferences and festivals in Texas, New Mexico, and Nevada. An editorial consultant for Linworth Publishing, Inc., she and her husband Donnie divide their time between the mountains of New Mexico and the beaches of South Texas.